Defending the Land

CULTURAL SURVIVAL STUDIES IN ETHNICITY AND CHANGE

Allyn & Bacon

Series Editors, David Maybury-Lewis and Theodore Macdonald, Jr.
Cultural Survival, Inc., Harvard University

Indigenous Peoples, Ethnic Groups, and the State, by David Maybury-Lewis

Malaysia and the "Original People": A Case Study of the Impact of Development on Indigenous Peoples, by Robert Knox Dentan, et al.

Gaining Ground? Evenkis, Land, and Reform in Southeastern Siberia, by Gail A. Fondahl

Ariaal Pastoralists of Kenya: Surviving Drought and Development in Africa's Arid Lands, by Elliot Fratkin

Defending the Land: Sovereignty and Forest Life in James Bay Cree Society, by Ronald Niezen

Forest Dwellers, Forest Protectors: Indigenous Models for International Development, by Richard Reed

Defending the Land: Sovereignty and Forest Life in James Bay Cree Society

Ronald Niezen
Harvard University

Allyn and Bacon
Boston • London • Toronto • Sydney • Tokyo • Singapore

Series Editor: Sarah L. Dunbar
Editor-in-Chief, Social Science: Karen Hanson
Series Editorial Assistant: Elissa V. Schaen
Marketing Manager: Karon Bowers
Consulting Editor: Sylvia Shepard
Manufacturing Buyer: Suzanne Lareau
Cover Administrator: Suzanne Harbison
Cover Designer: Jenny Hart
Editorial-Production Service: Omegatype Typography, Inc.

ISBN: 0-205-27580-X

Printed in the United States of America.
10   9   8   7   6   5   4   3   2   1   02   01   00   99   98   97

Photo credits: Photo 6.1 credited to Gretchen McHugh.
All other photographs are credited to
Ronald Niezen.

To Barbro

Contents

Foreword... ix

Acknowledgments... xi

Introduction... I

Living on the Land.. 13
    'OWNERSHIP' OF THE LAND 15
    SEASONS ON THE LAND 18
    FOREST SPIRITUALITY... 25
    HEALING... 31

The Origins of a Dual Lifestyle................................... 37
    THE FUR TRADE... 39
    MISSIONS, MEDICINE, AND
        RESIDENTIAL EDUCATION 41
    FEDERAL INTERVENTION 53

Negotiated Transformations 63
    HYDRO-ELECTRICITY AND THE GOALS OF
        EXTRACTIVE INDUSTRY... 65
    THE JAMES BAY AGREEMENT 68

Crisis and Accommodation... 81
    THE SOCIAL AFTERMATH... 84
    THE PURSUIT OF HEALTH CARE AUTONOMY 95

REDEFINING EDUCATION..102
ACCOMMODATION 106

Struggles over Sovereignty.. 113
THE JAMES BAY PROJECT REVISITED 116
TWO SOVEREIGNTIES 121
'THE SPOILERS' 126

Conclusion.. 135

References 140

Foreword to the Series

Cultural Survival is an organization founded in 1972 to defend the human rights of indigenous peoples, who are those, like the Indians of the Americas, who have been dominated and marginalized by peoples different from themselves. Since the states that claim jurisdiction over indigenous peoples consider them aliens and inferiors, they are among the world's most underprivileged minorities, facing a constant threat of physical extermination and cultural annihilation. This is no small matter, for indigenous peoples make up approximately five percent of the world's population. Most of them wish to become successful ethnic minorities, meaning that they be permitted to maintain their own traditions even though they are out of the mainstream in the countries where they live. Indigenous peoples hope therefore for multi-ethnic states that will tolerate diversity in their midst. In this their cause is the cause of ethnic minorities worldwide and is one of the major issues of our times, for the vast majority of states in the world are multi-ethnic. The question is whether states are able to recognize and live peaceably with ethnic differences, or whether they will treat them as an endless source of conflict.

Cultural Survival works to promote multi-ethnic solutions to otherwise conflictive situations. It sponsors research, advocacy, and publications which examine situations of ethnic conflict, especially (but not exclusively) as they affect indigenous peoples, and suggests solutions for them. It also provides technical and legal assistance to indigenous peoples and organizations.

This series of monographs entitled *The Cultural Survival Studies in Ethnicity and Change* is published in collaboration with Allyn & Bacon (the Simon and Schuster Education Group). It will focus on problems of ethnicity in the modern world and how they affect the interrelations between indigenous peoples, ethnic groups, and the state.

The studies will focus on the situations of ethnic minorities and of indigenous peoples, who are a special kind of ethnic minority, as they try to defend their rights, their resources, and their ways of life within modern states. Some of the volumes in the series will deal with general themes, such as ethnic conflict, indigenous rights, socio-economic development, or multiculturalism. These volumes will contain brief case studies to illustrate their general arguments. Meanwhile the series as a whole plans to publish a larger number of books that deal in depth with specific cases. It is our conviction that good case studies are essential for a better understanding of issues that arouse such passion in the world today and this series will provide them. Its emphasis nevertheless will be on relating the particular to the general in the comparative contexts of national or international affairs.

The books in the series will be short, averaging approximately 160 pages in length, and written in a clear and accessible style aimed at students and the general reader. They are intended to clarify issues that are often obscure or misunderstood and that are not treated succinctly elsewhere. It is our hope therefore that they will also prove useful as reference works for scholars and policy makers.

David Maybury-Lewis
Theodore Macdonald, Jr.
Cultural Survival, Inc.
96 Mt. Auburn St., 2nd Floor
Cambridge, Massachusetts 02138
(617) 441-5400 fax: (617) 441-5417
email: csinc@cs.org
website: www.cs.org

Acknowledgments

My first debt of gratitude is to the many Cree people who contributed openly and generously to several research projects under the auspices of the Cree Board of Health and Social Services of James Bay. The Cree Health Board hired me in 1987 and asked that I visit the (then) eight Cree communities as part of a project investigating the needs and activities of their social service branch. In April, 1992 I returned after being invited to participate in the spring caribou hunt; and from June–September, 1992, and July–August, 1993 I was invited to conduct interviews on traditional healing in Chisasibi and Mistissini. This work was supplemented by visits during 'goose-break' in May, 1994 and October, 1995. During these stays, the Cree Health Board assisted by arranging interviews and providing my accommodation, and funding was provided by the Clark Fund and Milton Fund of Harvard University. James Bobbish, General Manager of the Cree Health Board, was instrumental in encouraging this work and coming out with important insights during our 'power lunches' at Chisasibi's arena restaurant. During several of these visits, Sam Kitty and William Cromarty gave me memorable introductions to hunting activities. The James Bay Telecommunications Society made an important contribution to this research in the form of recorded interviews with elders from the weekly radio program, *Chischaiyu Aitimuun*, "the mind of an elder". Annie House, translator for the Youth Court, provided excellent translations of these narratives from the difficult Cree of elders into English. Funding for this translation project was generously provided by the Milton Fund of the Harvard Medical School. In the summer of 1996, the Nishnawbe-Aski Nation provided me with an important comparative experience by asking me to visit six Cree and Ojibwa communities in northern Ontario as part of a mental health policy development program. Although very little material from this project found its way into the present volume, it was significant in broadening my understanding of the situations and struggles of native peoples in the North. Support during the writing of the manuscript, in the form of a paper-storm of documents, was provided by Robert Epstein and Ann Stewart. The frontispiece map was produced through the persistent effort and remarkable computer skill of Arlene Olivero at the Harvard Map Collection. I am grateful to those colleagues who read and commented upon my work at several stages of completion, David Maybury-Lewis, Arthur Kleinman, and Arnold Devlin, and to Sylvia Shepard whose editorial insights were useful in the final revision. This work would have been impossible, or at least a lot less pleasant, without the personal support of my wife, Barbro, and sons Erik and Alexander, who were patient while I was away in the North, and even more patient when they came with me.

Introduction

> On the crucial question of the evolution of human society
> [Soviet ethnologist Dimitrii Ol'derogge] observed to me that
> whilst the base line and the terminus were the same for all man-
> kind, the paths of development between them were endlessly
> various.
>
> Ernest Gellner, 'Academician Ol'derogge'.

If we look carefully at what has motivated research done
among indigenous peoples during at least the past century,
we usually find a fear and expectation that all societies will
soon resemble one another. Whenever remote regions have
been opened up to exploration, development, and settlement,
the people living there, defeated in one way or another by
technology and addictions, are destined to disappear, to die
from disease or vice or fade from view in a quiet imitation of
the intruders' way of life. Disappearing with them are meaningful social differences. There is always a strong segment of
the colonizing society that approves of the assimilation or
extinction of 'savages', either out of a well-intentioned desire
to save their souls or a covetous zeal to acquire their land and
its riches. But researchers and students of ethnography often
work with a sense of loss at the prospect of cultural extinction
as they set themselves the task of preservation, the kind of
preservation that uses the methods of observation and analy-
sis to record everything about the native way of life before it

is gone forever. At the same time, social theorists have sometimes used ethnographic observations to arrive at the general conclusion that human societies are becoming increasingly similar, organized around industrialism, the nuclear family, and the powerful forces of bureaucracy and technological specialization. 'Tribalism' or 'traditional societies' are becoming marginalized or are already part of this new social order.

In its extreme form, the view that cultures or ways of life are destined to become similar in values, standards of virtue, and definitions of reality is referred to by Ernest Gellner as the convergence thesis. He describes this rather bleak processes of modernization as a movement toward universal cultural uniformity:

> Suppose it *were* indeed the case that the industrial mode of production uniquely determines the culture of society: the same technology canalizes people into the same type of activity and the same kinds of hierarchy, and that the same kind of leisure styles were also engendered by the existing techniques and by the needs of productive life. Diverse languages might and probably would, of course, survive: but the social uses to which they were being put, the meanings available in them, would be much the same in any language within this wider shared industrial culture (1983: 116).

Gellner is describing the terminus of human history related to him by Dimitrii Ol'derogge in the epigraph to this introduction, an image derived from the expectation that all human societies will one day resemble one another in their basic institutional organization, use of technology, and cultural outlook.

This book is about a people who have largely succeeded in defying such a pattern of cultural homogenization, at least for the present and the foreseeable future. Having been challenged with missions, boarding schools, massive hydroelectric construction, village relocation, and other agents of rapid cultural change, the James Bay Cree of northern Québec have not only maintained basic connections to a hunting, fishing, and trapping lifestyle, but have at the same time become significant players in the 'politics of embarrassment', pushing for greater native regional autonomy while resisting the threats of major resource development and Québec's sovereignty movement. The Cree have created a bridge between their forest lifestyle and the demands of administrative development and political struggle, between tradition and bureaucracy.

The transitions that have taken place for the 12,000 Crees of Québec's James Bay region during the past several decades have been, by any standard, tumultuous. Although federal involvement in native affairs after World War Two encouraged settlement in villages for administrative purposes, most families followed the long established pattern of gathering in communities only in the summer months. Until the early-1970s there was only sporadic and informal contact between the Cree leaders of widely scattered communities. Then in 1972, the Québec government of Premier Bourassa announced its plans for the construction of a $6 billion project on the La Grande River with no prior consultation with the Cree who claimed the region as ancestral territory. A union of Cree leaders was quickly mobilized and legal opposition to the project mounted. A victory for the Cree, who placed a moratorium on construction until native claims could be resolved, was overturned on appeal in Québec Superior Court only one week later. The temporary legal success, and the promise of more legal action to come, prompted the Québec government, together with the federal government and Cree and Inuit representatives, to negotiate the James Bay and Northern Québec Agreement. This Agreement provided the Québec government with jurisdiction over lands on which the Hydro-Québec project was to be constructed (in fact construction had begun well in advance of court action) and administrative inclusion of Cree and Inuit communities into the provincial system. Besides the key issues of land allocation and case settlement (today amounting to $255 million), the Cree negotiated a plan for regional autonomy in education, health care and the Income Security Program, the latter providing a guaranteed income to hunters and their families who spend most of their time in the forest.

The impact of the implementation of the James Bay Agreement, which began in the late 1970s, is still being felt. The Cree were given control and responsibility for major institutions at a time when Hydro-Québec construction and flooding were forcing major adjustments to forest life. In Fort George, the community that has been the focus of my work, relocation to a site renamed Chisasibi ('big river') brought with it great emotional stress at a time when the social services was operating in a fledgling native organization.

Scarcely had these crises been faced when the Québec government and Hydro-Québec announced plans for further, massive hydro-electric projects on the Great Whale River and the Nottaway-Broadback-Rupert River System. Cree opposition to these projects brought a relatively new, untested leadership into the international arena. Lobbying efforts to halt the Great Whale project, the first of the new developments to be implemented, focused on communicating the Cree point of view to the people of the United States, to whom most of the power was to be exported.

For the Québec government, native regional autonomy was found to be a two-edged sword. While it did indeed include native administration in the Québec system, intended in part to elevate the province's profile, improving its claim to nationhood as a government that can deal with indigenous affairs, it did not succeed in cultivating a relationship uniformly based upon cooperation with native leaders.

This continues to have significant consequences for Québec's sovereignty movement. The sour experiences of the implementation of the James Bay Agreement, the hydro-electric construction, and the bitter struggle over the proposed Great Whale project convinced Cree leaders and the vast majority of their constituents to resist the inclusion of their communities and lands in a sovereign Québec, challenging the territorial integrity of the region that Québec sovereigntists claim as an inviolable national unity.

For many years, relations between native and non-native governments in Canada and elsewhere have been characterized by the politics of embarrassment, the use of media and public relations to expose the inconsistencies and injustices of government action. This relationship is predicated on bringing to the attention of a largely sympathetic audience of voting constituents, the injustice, bigotry and impact of the government's negligence on the living conditions in native communities. Once government agencies and individuals have been identified as being responsible for a crisis situation in native communities, then action (or inaction) comes under careful scrutiny by native leaders and the media.

The James Bay Cree of Québec have used the politics of embarrassment effectively, pointing mainly to the ill-considered social and environmental consequences of hydro-electric development and government foot-dragging in the implementation of the James Bay Agreement. The Cree struggle against their possible inclusion in a sovereign Québec shows that wider issues of national and international significance can come under the purview of relatively small indigenous populations. The politics of embarrassment have expanded to include the sympathies and judgments of the international community.

The Cree response to hydro-electric development and the James Bay Agreement, however, is not really about the successful duplication of non-native administrations, political strategies and social values. Cree hunters have long used tools invented and manufactured outside their own society. Breech-loading carbine rifles or outboard motors did not undermine basic attachments to the land or erode spiritual relationships with hunted animals. Similarly, though on a larger scale, the development of Cree administrations based on southern models does not in itself mean that their values, goals, and strategies will be the same as those of parent organizations in non-native societies. Although the goal of regional autonomy, as seen from the view of government negotiators, was a closer integration of the Cree in the Québec administrative system, from the Cree point of view it also provided opportunities for reinvigorating attachments to forest life.

Ironically, the bedrock of the expanding political profile of the Cree leadership is the forest economy, with camps usually joining several families scattered through a vast expanse of sub-arctic wilderness, nearly equalling the area of the state of Montana. Isolation is a matter of perception, a sense of discomfort arising out of distance from human companionship that can occur almost anywhere. For Cree hunters, however, there seems to be little loneliness, even in solitude of the land. The hunting, fishing, and trapping way of life is one of the threads of continuity that has made the forest so important to Cree culture, giving impulse to both the local struggle for subsistence and the politics of international recognition. Cree language, with its great precision in representing natural phenomena and human activity, is the foundation of Cree cultural curriculum in the primary grades of village schools. Attachment to forest life is the source of recent efforts to reform the administration of justice, social services, and health care to make them more consistent with indigenous understanding of conflict resolution and a holistic approach to emotional and physical well-being. And it is the most convincing source of the claim that the Cree people of the James Bay are a distinct society with equal or greater claim to sovereignty and self-determination than Québec's francophone community.

This book aims to correct two basic misconceptions of Cree Society as they relate to efforts to incorporate formal administrations into a culture that identifies closely with a quintessentially informal forest economy based on hunting, fishing, and trapping. The first misconception has its roots in the basic argument that bureaucrats and hunters don't mix. The logic of this model implies the erosion of tradition as an organizing principle of human behavior wherever it comes into contact with bureaucratic powers. For some, centralized politics and the rapid development of a wide range of bureaucratic institutions spells the decline of traditional values: obedience based on respect and continuity of the knowledge and authority of elders. Cree regional autonomy is, according to this view, the newest, and most effective form of cultural assimilation. Indigenous societies like the Cree, in which a respect for elders and the social intimacy of forest camps are being altered by village settlement and administrative inclusions into government agencies, have, according to this view, little chance for cultural survival. This view has been a major impulse behind government policies which aimed to hasten assimilation to make inevitable transformations less painful.

A variation of this view emphasizes the erosive impact of technology. Western-trained amateur and professional observers alike are easily caught up in the romance of living close to the land, fatally susceptible to finding what is lacking in their own lives and cultural heritage, rather than what is or is not present in the daily life of the camp. Imported technology becomes seen as a sure sign of cultural decline when cultural integrity is defined by the use and retention of only locally-manufactured items. But for the Cree, several key manufactured items have become central to the continued viability of the forest lifestyle. Transport to and from remote camps was a seasonal activity, with travel by canoe taking several weeks to a month in the Spring and Fall; now it is made much easier and less seasonal with the availability of planes, automobiles, snowmobiles, 'four-wheelers', and motorboats. Shotguns for small game and waterfowl and breech-loading repeating rifles for large game have greatly improved hunting success. Chain saws make it easier to construct cabins and maintain the supply of firewood. In all these instances, forest life is more often enhanced, rather than compromised, by the manufactured item. The only value intrinsically violated by such uses of technology is the non-native observer's sense of the picturesque. The forest life of Cree camps is easily romanticized by those looking for signs of a connection with the environment they have lost, but it has not remained unchanged by such things as road construction or new technologies in hunting, trapping, medicine, and communication. Even discarded building supplies left over from dam projects in the early 1990s resulted almost instantly in more permanent and comfortable cabins in many of the camps accessible by road. The forest way of life has a long history of accommodation and innovation resulting from outside influence. And while the usual way of perceiving this relationship is to see the camps as the furthest outposts of influence from 'civilization' there is a great willingness to accept and to initiate change within the limits of practicality.

A political misconception of the implications of administration stresses an opposite danger. Indigenous peoples' uses
of administrations are seen to be too effective in their defense
of local culture, providing them with both a distinct identity
and the means to pursue radical political objectives. The central concern here is not cultural survival but the political outcome of regional autonomy and recognition of sovereignty.
While the expression of this idea occurred in the context of
Québec's political maneuvering in the international arena, it
would not have been put forth if some members of the government and the public were not ready to believe it. During
the 1995 Québec sovereignty debate, which was leading to a
referendum on independence, *Québécois* nationalists created
the image of indigenous societies the world over following
the lead of politically savvy indigenous groups within their
own province, making bids for status as distinct nations, pursuing radical autonomy, creating political turmoil. Here the
potential of Cree institutions was more realistically portrayed
while the actual political objectives of the Cree leadership
were, perhaps purposefully, misconstrued. Cree leaders, as
we will see in more detail in Chapter 5, used their rights of
self-determination to make a claim for inclusion in the federal
system, rather than for their own independent statehood.
Apart from the political maneuvering of this conflict over the
intentions of Cree sovereignty, the mistake is easy to make.
The Cree have developed a political organization that in
many ways resembles the ethnic nationalism so feared or
hoped for in other parts of the world. Their self-reference as a
'Cree Nation', with an 'embassy' in Ottawa can be misunderstood as the outward trappings of a strong proto-nationalism,
not to mention (as we do later on) many of the referents of
local identity and sovereignty that fit equally well with schol-
arly descriptions of nationalist movements. But the principal
goal of Cree sovereignty is a fair, equitable, carefully negotiated and honored inclusion in an already existing state—Canada—rather than an independent nation. The Cree provide the
interesting example of a nationalism within a nation, running
counter to the common perception of ethnic nationalism as
driven by goals of secession.

A variation of this theme involves an attempt to discredit the place of Cree leaders as stewards of the land. The Cree are keepers of the land in name only, this argument runs, but give them the control they seek and they will pursue industrial development as ambitiously and destructively as any of their free enterprise adversaries. In a brief filed with the International Water Tribunal in Amsterdam in February, 1992, for example, Jacques Finet, vice-president of Hydro-Québec, accused the Cree of using their concerns for the environment and native society as a way of gaining sympathy in a fight for ownership of the James Bay and its resources. "It wouldn't be six months before you would see bulldozers in the area if it was their country and they had control over natural resources" (*Gazette*, 1992a) Indigenous motives for ecological balance and stewardship of the land are seen as smoke screens for concealed ambitions toward power and profit.

Although based on a politically motivated attempt to discredit the Cree leadership in its bid to control forest resources, this argument points to an important feature of Cree society: village centralization and a rapidly growing population mean that a declining minority can successfully live from forest resources by hunting, fishing, and trapping. A pivotal challenge for present and future leaders is to encourage the viability and integrity of the forest-way of life, while ensuring communication of its cultural values to a village population with fewer ties to the land. It is also faced with finding meaningful activity and employment for a population living in remote villages. This situation is a basis for those who say that, given greater control of natural resources, the Cree leadership would pursue identical strategies of land use as non-native private enterprise.

If we take the themes I have just described and render them into even more basic components, we arrive at a pair of opposites with administration and technology as the defining issues. Those who stress cultural differences between Cree and Euro-Canadian societies see bureaucratic institutions and technology as threats to the distinct lifestyle of the Cree, even under conditions of regional administrative autonomy. This perception fits well with a romanticized under-standing of the forest lifestyle that stresses its incompatibility with technology and village life.

The opposite argument strategically aligns the Cree with particular currents in non-native society. Québec sovereign-tists raise the fear that the Cree want to pursue indepen-dence; those interested in resource extraction raise concerns that what Cree leaders really want is to extract resources for profit. In almost classic examples of projection, Cree society becomes mirrored into a form identical to that of its critics, with identical political and economic goals lying beneath as-sertions of unique cultural identity.

The Cree people are a special case because such a wide gulf between contrasting perceptions can develop. In most indigenous societies this does not occur; and the view that predicts political and cultural disaster would be closer to the truth. It is still very common to find aboriginal peoples with-out recognized claims to land, resources, or identity. The Cree themselves were able to resist this degree of centralized political domination by negotiating for control of land and administrations, and by successfully maneuvering through the legal and political institutions of Euro-Canadian society in defense of unique interests in and uses of the land.

Rather than try to steer a course between these two views, I will present a view of Cree 'ethnicity' that accepts some of their premises, but differs from them in fundamen-tal ways. The approach that stresses cultural differences and fragility is correct in the sense that forces of acculturation and political domination have exerted extreme pressures on Cree society, posing threats above all to the forest lifestyle and the teachings that follow from it. Too often, however, it is only the stories of cultural decline that are emphasized in contemporary accounts of native societies, and too often the social pathologies are dwelt upon in showing the down-ward spirals of communities broken by apathy and despair. And while many of these stories are true and instructive and deserve to elicit our sympathy, we are often left with a sense that little can be accomplished other than to chronicle tragic situations and perhaps convince politicians and the public that irreversible injustices have been committed. Not enough credit is given to formally educated native leaders, elders, and involved community members for attempting to arrest the spiral, regain control of local decision making, and work to restore 'health' in the broad sense that it is usually locally understood. When communities have truly succumbed to lifestyles encouraging depression, violence, and self-destruction, the interruption of the processes of active leadership and healing also occurs. But a society can survive great hardship if it is left with the abilities to resist and to heal.

It is misleading to focus on domination and social pathology without also considering the local response to social crisis. Cree resistance to large-scale development, the negotiation of regional autonomy in the James Bay Agreement, and subsequent adjustments to new administrations provide examples of indigenous activism changing the rules of political engagement with non-native society, responding to social crisis, trying to accommodate rapid social change with a sense of order and continuity. Without telling this part of the story very little of Cree society can be properly understood.

2

Living on the Land

I have heard a clergyman...say that...when any one of [the Indians from his Parish] in summer has been absent for some weeks a-hunting, he comes back among them a different person and altogether unlike any of the rest, with an eagle's eye, a wild look, and commanding carriage and gesture.

Ralph Waldo Emerson,
The Heart of Emerson's Journals.

Almost anyone would agree that sleeping ten adults and eight children from three families in a twelve by twenty-foot cabin has the potential to create an intense social experience, but this is a normal arrangement for Cree families living on the land. If there are petty irritations or resentments in the Cree camp, they rarely show; people seem to be unshakably even-tempered. When his van broke down while gathering firewood several miles from camp in –20° Fahrenheit with a biting wind, Sam Bearskin,[1] an experienced hunter in his fifties, gave no indication of being bothered. He seemed oblivious when trucks from the hydro-electric projects drove past in swirls of powdery snow and calmly, nearly an hour later, accepted a ride from a well-intentioned tourist some 200

---

1. The names of individuals referred to in this book have been changed, with the frequent exception of those who at some time occupied positions of leadership.

yards from his destination, up the short access road leading to his camp. Inside the cabin (*muhtukan*),[2] children were warned not to go near the hot barrel-stove and scolded when they became too rambunctious, but anger did not show in anyone's voice, echoing what Willis writes about her upbringing in Fort George, "While they might click their tongues, shake their heads sadly, or occasionally threaten, our parents were never very strict with us" (1973: 97). No one complained of sleeplessness from lack of room or from the cold as the fire died down leaving breath-crystals to form on the bedding. In the morning, Sam, the owner of the cabin and its surrounding hunting territory, woke before dawn to start the fire. Plans for the day were confirmed over breakfast. Some of the young people would be taken to a patch of willows on the lakeshore to set rabbit snares. Someone else would drive to town with Sam to arrange for his van to be towed and repaired. With a much-anticipated caribou hunt postponed, nobody expressed disappointment or remarked that rabbit-snaring would be a poor substitute.

Such calm in the face of disappointment, hardship, and potential danger is not an isolated phenomenon. Forest life is recognized throughout Cree society as a potential source of personal improvement. "When I did something wrong, I would go back in the bush and correct myself.... That was our teaching taught by our elders.... [When] I knew I was not going in the right direction, I would correct myself, go out there and find myself."[3] Before the establishment of formal helping agencies, Isaac Schecapio, chief of the inland community of Mistassini in the 1930s, had the responsibility of resolving interpersonal problems in a rapidly growing village that brought families from widely scattered hunting territories together in a central location for the first time. He would intervene in marriage difficulties by sending couples out to a remote camp, with only enough provisions to get

---

2. Unless otherwise noted, the Cree orthography used in this book follows the method of the Cree Lexicon (Cree School Board, 1987).

3. Unless otherwise noted, interviews were conducted by the author in English.

them started before the fall freeze-up. When these couples returned to the community the next summer, their problems had usually been resolved. Robbie Matthew, Sr. of Chisasibi remembers his father helping an elder with severe emotional problems by taking him out on the land: "A person's mind is awake out there. And [the elder] had to get back in touch with himself. What [my father] used was the land.... After a while [the elder] was in a different state.... He could talk. He could really picture himself as a new person."

What, to the Cree, is so important about 'the bush', 'nuh-chimiihch'? In what sense can the land be 'owned'? What makes activity there part of a healing process? None of the recent political actions of Cree leaders in national and international forums can be understood without considering these questions. Cree defense of the land takes on new meaning when we consider such things as the spiritual relationship between hunters and their quarry, the hardships faced within living memory in remote traplines, the knowledge and self-reliance needed to be successful and support a family, and the ability some people still have to use products of the land as medicine.

'OWNERSHIP' OF THE LAND

In 1670 a British Royal Charter granted the Hudson's Bay Company rights to ownership and governance over a vast portion of subarctic North America. With Canadian confederation in 1867, sovereignty and proprietorship in the subarctic were partitioned between federal and provincial governments through a succession of constitutional and legislative processes. None of these events were taken notice of by the Cree hunters of the North. Their occupation of the land was not based upon unrestricted proprietary rights, but upon the technical and social aspects of managing hunting, fishing, and trapping activities. Colin Scott describes the Cree approach to property as deriving from customary rights that are socially mediated: "living resources and products may be specified, but these relate to the technical and political relations of managing and sharing resources"

(1988: 40). Harvey Feit shows that early studies of Algonquin hunting territories, particularly those by Frank Speck, misinterpreted the social meaning of 'ownership', presenting a model that too closely approximated formal concepts of 'property', prompted by a desire to defend native interests in the face of non-native alienation of land. Speck's error was in not adequately portraying the rights and duties tied to notions of reciprocity and egalitarian leadership that are involved in the 'ownership' of hunting territories (Feit, 1991). Control of areas of land and its resources is a conditional form of authority derived from social recognition of skills and responsibilities rather than an exchange or purchase that confers exclusive, binding rights of possession.

Two long-standing principles of the rights and obligations associated with land use in Cree society are stewardship and sharing. A steward or 'tallyman' (*uuchimaau*) is responsible for a designated hunting territory. There is some evidence that management of specific territories by 'principal Indians' (as fur traders referred to them) is a situation of long standing in the eastern James Bay. Daniel Francis and Toby Morantz find that when Hudson's Bay Company Governor George Simpson wrote to his superiors in London in 1828 stating his intention to implement distinct hunting grounds, the eastern James Bay Cree already had them. "[T]he roots of such a land tenure system seem to go back at least to the early 1700s and the presence in the records of clearly worded references to such a system already in existence predate the company's stated intentions [to implement individually owned hunting territories]" (Francis and Morantz 1983: 127).

Despite the formalization of hunting territories as a result of the James Bay Agreement in the 1970s, the principal obligations of the hunting leader have remained unchanged to the present. The *uuchimaau* fulfills his responsibility by coordinating the activities of families using the 'trapline,' ensuring that particular species of animals (especially beaver, the focus of fur-trade activity) are not overharvested and that the widely scattered camps are bringing in enough food to meet everyone's needs. Some hunting leaders are specialists because of their skill in coordinating a particular activity, such as the caribou hunt. More permanent and wide-ranging stewardship of a 'trapline' (not, strictly speaking a 'line' at all, but an area of land or 'territory'), is a privilege inherited from an elder hunter, usually an agnatic kinsman, but occasionally a maternal uncle or unrelated mentor, whose special relationship with a young man will involve education in the responsibilities of being a custodian of the hunter's territory. As one hunter recalled, the process of taking responsibility for a trapline did not involve a formal transaction: "My uncle handed down the land to me as his elders had handed it down to him. He gave me the land to look after it; he did not sell me the land or ask for anything in return" (Cree Trappers Association, 1989: 9). Another elder recalls the advice that was given to him when he accepted stewardship of a territory: "It is up to you to protect, preserve, make rules where necessary and enforce good hunting practices. You will look after it as I have shown you in the past. You will also look after your people and share what you have on the land if they are willing to practice their way of life" (Cree Trappers Association, 1989: 9). 'Ownership' of land is attached to social responsibilities that emphasize hunting expertise, leadership ability, and sharing.

At the same time, coordination of forest activities could not take place without cooperation from the hunters using the land. Some hunting families are more mobile than others, extending their activities through several territories. Trapline owners need to be informed of their plans for using an area and grant permission for their stay. Normally, travelling through a trapline *en route* to a camp in another region, relying temporarily on the staple resources of small game and fish, does not require a prior statement of intention and permission of the 'hunting boss'.

No *uuchimaau* would long retain his status if he mismanaged through incompetence or attempted to hoard resources in a bid to accumulate political control. The Cree, like other egalitarian foraging societies, place more emphasis on adaptability to the land rather than accumulation, and breeches of etiquette are handled more by ridicule and social isolation than punishment. "If the hunting boss fails as a steward or sharer of resources, others will soon use his grounds without permission and coordination. His ability to manage resources will decline, and another territory boss will sooner or later be recognized by the hunting group and by the wider Cree community" (Scott, 1988: 39). This was especially true before the greater formalization of hunting territories that accompanied the James Bay and Northern Québec Agreement of 1975. 'Stewardship' (*nitihaaihtaan*) of the land is inseparable from a social recognition of competence in coordinating hunting activity and redistributing products of the hunt.

SEASONS ON THE LAND

The view from any high point in the land surrounding Chisasibi reveals a black spruce forest interspersed with jack pine and tamarack, stunted by the short growing season of some sixty days without frost, stretching to the horizon in a seemingly uninterrupted expanse of coniferous green. Viewed from the air, the same landscape tells a different story. The trees are seen to be frequently interrupted by lakes, marshes, streams, and rivers in an intricate hydrological maze, made all the more complex by the aimless meandering of minor waterways finding their way across the flat, recently glaciated landscape, eventually forming tributaries of the great rivers that drain into the Hudson Bay and James Bay.[4] Before the construction of roads and dams, rivers were principal travel routes, usable only between the spring thaw and fall 'freeze-up'. During summer, away from the principal waterways, the traveller often faces impenetrable bogs. With the changing of seasons, travel patterns are reversed. In fall and spring, in the times of freeze-up and break-up, the many bodies of water themselves act as an impediment to movement because the weak ice obstructs canoe travel but cannot support much weight. Moving unimpeded across the land is possible only when the lakes, marshes, and bogs are frozen. In winter conditions the land opens up

---

4. See Gardner (1981) for a more detailed study of the subarctic environment.

and, equipped with a good pair of snowshoes, a dog sled, or a snowmobile, a person who knows the land can go almost anywhere. A few of the elders in the Cree villages can talk about trips they took overland from the James Bay coast to Labrador, travelling from camp to camp, welcomed as a guest, and given directions for the next leg of the journey.

For those inexperienced with the cold, however, the winters are unforgiving. Temperatures of −40° Fahrenheit in January are not uncommon, and with a stiff wind blowing inland from the bay the wind-chill factor can add to the risk of exposure. Snow cover lasts for nearly 200 days a year. Despite the position of Chisasibi on roughly the same 53° latitude as Belfast, Ireland, winter weather in the James Bay region is much more extreme. Prevailing arctic wind currents are funneled down the Hudson Bay, adding to severe temperatures and snow accumulation. The same winds redistribute the light snow of the boreal forest, clearing lakes and hill tops, while forming deep drifts in hollows and the leeward sides of forest edges.

Human activity revolves around these dramatically contrasting seasons. In the time before children were required to attend school in the villages, the summer, from June to August or September, was the only time of the year when people gathered in a community. Summer was a socially active time of year, with a constant round of visits between households. Women used this time to make such things as mittens, moccasins, and rabbit skin coats while men whittled with crooked knives (drawing knives with a curved blade) to make canoe paddles or narrow shovels for clearing snow around traps or fishing holes in the ice. There were also more exclusively male gatherings at the Hudson's Bay post where, drinking from pails of home brew, hunters would talk until late at night.

During this season, fishing was one of the only productive subsistence activities. Trout and salmon were caught with nets on long poles at rapids as they swam upstream, sturgeon were speared in the shallows of fast-moving water, and whitefish could be gill-netted in large quantities in the rivers, providing a staple that was smoked or mixed with dried berries in pemmican, a concentrated food used widely by natives, explorers, and fur traders in the North. Beluga whales were once hunted in June and July as they migrated into coastal bays and inlets, sometimes even into the La Grande River itself. (The whales have not been seen in these waters, however, since the hydro-electric construction of the 1970s.) In preparation for the coming season on the land, trappers would take out advances from the trading posts to purchase the supplies they needed. For many years, beaver pelts were the currency used to measure the value of an item and a trapper's burden of debt.

In September, 'goose camps' would be set up along the James Bay coast to correspond with the semi-annual goose migration. When this was over, before freeze-up, many hunters moved inland to check beaver inventories and set up a winter camp. Some hunters from Chisasibi whose traplines were far inland would make journeys of several weeks by canoe. Travel against the current was slow and, as one elderly woman remembers, the need to portage around rapids, burdened with supplies and young children, made progress even more uneven: "During the portaging I used to tie both kids to trees, within reach of each other so they could play together. My husband used to carry our canoe and I carried our belongings; and on the last trip I carried one child and the other went with his dad."[5] Even before the ice became thick enough to travel on, there were still opportunities for hunting. Muskrats were trapped in the Fall and moose, most abundant in the southern Cree territories, would be in rut, making them less cautious and more active than usual.

---

5. This quotation from a female elder in Chisasibi is part of a collection of thirty-six interviews with Cree elders for the James Bay Telecommunications Society's weekly radio program "*chischaiyu aitimuun*," 'the mind of an elder', which began weekly broadcasts in 1992. The recordings were neither cataloged nor dated, but the translator of this material, Annie House, was able to identify most of the speakers and their community of origin. The value (and limitation) of these interviews stems from the fact that elders and other Cree interviewees are speaking for a Cree audience, communicating what they feel is important for community members to hear.

A winter lodge in April.

When the ice was secure, families would settle into winter camps. This was often the most solitary time of year. Families were dispersed to distribute their activity throughout a hunting territory. "It was rare that you saw people during the Winter. You see, everybody had their own section of the trapline, even if it was family-owned."[6] Men were often gone during the day to check traps, or away from the camp for weeks at a time in pursuit of hibernating black bear or the moose which foraged on the wind-swept crests of hills where the snow is not as deep. Women left to care for children and maintain the camp were kept busy with a variety of chores: collecting and splitting firewood, carrying water, preparing food, gathering and drying baby-moss to be

6. Excerpt from a radio narrative recorded in Chisasibi.

used as diapers for infants, laying fresh spruce-boughs on the floor of the cabin or teepee, and maintaining a supply of small game by snaring rabbits, shooting grouse and ptarmigans, and catching fish with night-lines or nets under the ice. Sometimes, when women were alone or with small children, these chores could not even be compromised by the event of childbirth:

> The men didn't stay put in the camp. They used to be gone a week at a time [looking for game]. Only my five-year-old daughter and myself were left in the camp. I chopped wood, lots of it, getting ready for my childbirth. Every day I gathered wood. Not far from our camp we had set our fish hooks. These needed daily attention, and it was up to me to check on them. This was my food to live on while the men were gone. [My labor] started when I was following the routine of gathering wood for the camp.... Still, I didn't stop working. About noon, I knew for sure I was in labor. I took wood into our teepee, enough to last for a while. Once inside, I put water on the stove and got things ready for the delivery. The only person there was my daughter. I didn't say anything to her. I lay myself down. It took only a few pushes and the baby was out. The thing that puzzled me is that the whole sack came out. I broke the sack and got her out, cut the umbilical cord, washed her, and bundled her up. After I finished with my baby, I lay down again and the placenta came. I cleaned myself up and did what had to be done. Later in the night the firewood that was inside was almost gone. I got myself dressed very warmly and brought more wood inside. In the morning I went to get water. During all this time, I didn't sleep. For eight days, I couldn't sleep. I kept the fire burning day and night. On the eighth day my husband and brother-in-law came home, and on the ninth day I finally went to sleep.[7]

---

7. Excerpt from a radio narrative recorded in Chisasibi.

Although conditions in even the most remote traplines have changed with the advent of such things as radio communication and air ambulances, stories like this are not uncommon, especially from those old enough to have lived through extended periods of true isolation in the winter camps.

For men, as an elder in Moose Factory recalls, the winter routine was also demanding: "They would wake up around three o'clock in the morning. By four o'clock they would leave the camp and only return at the end of the day.... When a young man would go out trapping all day he would take a pail with him, a small pail to make tea. And he would only stop to make one fire during that whole day."[8] Boys being raised in the forest were sometimes taken out to be left alone in the bush when they were ten, eleven, or twelve years old. They were usually left with an axe and some matches and asked to retrieve the beaver caught in traps and then to reset and replace the traps. Similar experiences of forest initiation took place during moose hunting in the inland communities. A youth worker in Mistassini told me how his seventy-year-old father killed his first moose at the age of twelve. When fresh tracks were found in the snow and the more experienced hunters knew a moose was not far off, they told him to track and kill the animal on his own. He approached it the way he had been taught, being especially careful of the direction the wind carried his scent, and eventually killed it with his .22 caliber rifle. He was left with the problem of what to do with the dead animal because he had not been taught how to prepare the carcass, and in any case was not strong enough to do it on his own. His solution was to cut off the ear and take it with him to the camp. The more experienced hunters accepted his token of success, then hurried off to bring back the carcass.

In spring it was sometimes necessary for families to move to areas where they could maintain a supply of game. Travelling to a new area in March was remembered as a

---

8. This interview in Cree took place in Moose Factory, Ontario on July 5, 1996 and was translated by Sam Sackanay.

sometimes arduous experience by an elder in Chisasibi: "This was the time of year when people were bothered by snow blindness, and still they walked to new locations. The person with snow blindness was put on a leash and used to walk behind someone who had the guide-line."[9] Early Spring, before the return of waterfowl along the coast and the later travel to the communities, was potentially a lean time of year. If hunters had been unsuccessful in finding big game over the winter, families would have to rely on fish, rabbits, and game birds to make it through the year. Each species goes through cycles of abundance and decline; and in some years their low populations would occur simultaneously, leading to starvation in remote camps.

> These were the hardest times I've known. There were lots of us in one camp. My younger brothers and sisters were crying because of hunger, but there was nothing to give them. One evening my mother saw my father walking across the [frozen] lake. I don't know how many times he sat down to get rest, due to the fact that he hadn't eaten a thing for the previous few days. I had arrived back at the camp a few minutes earlier. I had [killed] a few ptarmigans that day and my mother had them cooking in a pot where they were starting to make broth. I told my mother to put some broth in a pot that I would take to my father. He was still quite a distance away. I went to get him, took the soup to him to drink, and he felt better, but still I insisted that he get on the sled instead of walking, and I brought the sled right to the door.[10]

For younger generations, there is no equivalent experience of hardship. Yet the example of elders who survived through years of starvation in the early 1930s can be a reminder of the importance of maintaining a connection to the land: "There were times that our ancestors were starving…and yet they

---

9. Excerpt from a radio narrative recorded in Chisasibi
10. Excerpt from a radio narrative recorded in Chisasibi.

didn't give up the land…We've always maintained the faith that someday everything will turn out right. We've always trusted that the land will produce one day, that there will be enough for people to share." Stories of hardship do not encourage abandonment of forest life so much as admiration for the courage of survivors and appreciation of times when the land is plentiful.

FOREST SPIRITUALITY

The Cree understanding of how and why the land provides for its human inhabitants is to a surprising extent grounded in spiritual rather than material considerations. Writing in the 1930s of the Montagnais-Naskapi of the Labrador Peninsula and the people today called the Cree of Mistassini, Frank Speck made the interesting observation that "hunting is a holy occupation." (Speck, 1977: 72). His attention to forest spirituality, and in particular the drama of human-animal relationships, was a departure from the usual depiction of hunting peoples which tended to stress material aspects of subsistence strategies. Among Speck's findings was the origin of rules of conduct in spiritual concerns:

> failure in the chase, the disappearance of the game from the hunter's districts, with ensuing famine, starvation, weakness, sickness, and death, are all attributed to the hunter's ignorance of some hidden principles of behavior toward the animals, or to his willful disregard of them. The former is ignorance. The latter is sin (1977: 73).

More recently, Robert Brightman finds that such practices as communication with game animals in dreams, and showing ritual respect toward animals that are killed continue to be central to human-animal relationships among Cree hunters of northern Manitoba. He describes the spirituality of the forest lifestyle as situated in a number of contradictory, contextually variable qualities attributed to animals: subject to reincarnation, yet finite; powerful, yet vulnerable; capable of both friendship and almost malicious opposition. Animals are spiritually powerful beings that can 'offer' themselves to the hunter or conceal themselves and obstruct the hunt; and animal behavior is linked to a spiritual relationship with humans that must be cultivated by ritual activity and symbolic exchange. Such perceptions, he argues, are every bit as important in determining human behavior as more purely instrumental or economic concerns. For Brightman, Cree productive activity is itself part of a symbolic understanding of human-animal relationships in an ecosystem that is a social construction: "Society embraces rather than excludes animals, and the events of killing and eating them are experienced and talked about as so many ongoing instances of social interaction" (1993: 2).

In another line of interpretation Brightman considers the historical variability of Cree hunting activities and relationships with the natural world. Using evidence of Cree hunting practices from reports and journals of the Hudson's Bay Company from the nineteenth century, he argues that Algonquin hunters of the boreal forest during the early fur trade lacked a western conception of the finitude of animal species and the 'management' of game. The number of caribou killed in a hunt, for example, sometimes far exceeded the subsistence needs of hunters. Brightman explains this with reference to ambiguous symbolic relationships between hunters and prey, belief in animal reincarnation, and the corresponding absence of the idea that the number of animals can decline significantly through human activity. "The dominant ideology of human-animal relationships," Brightman writes, "not only allowed indiscriminate hunting, but enjoined it." 'Respect,' in other words, was not originally conjoined with technical management in the way that it is in some subarctic Indian communities today" (1993: 290).

Spiritual relationships between hunters and their quarry, however, continue to exist among many experienced Cree hunters today, in a form that is far from 'technical'. While I was visiting the Matthew family in Chisasibi during the Summer of 1994, Robbie Matthew, Sr. asked his wife Sally to remove the esophagus of a goose she was preparing, then explained to me what was done with it. The esophagus of a goose is hung on a tree at every hunt to pay respect to the animal. The windpipe is the most important part because this is where the voice of the goose is from. He expressed regret that some hunters didn't do this and that some young people had even been seen shooting at geese from a vehicle. This, he said, could mean declining numbers of geese for the community in the future.

The reason improper hunting behavior was a concern was not because too many geese would be killed this way, leading to a reduction in the goose population. (In fact, shooting from a car is in general not an effective strategy for goose-hunting.) It was because the spiritual relationship between hunters and a symbolically important animal had been compromised, and the quarry was likely to respond by making itself unavailable. As one member of a panel of hunters in Chisasibi explains, "A hunter always speaks as if the animals are in control of the hunt. The success of the hunt depends on the animals: The hunter is successful if the animal decides to make himself available. The hunters have no power over the game; animals have the last say as to whether they will be caught" (Cree Trappers Association, 1989: 21). Respect for animals is therefore not a mere appendage to one's skill as a hunter. Success in the forest economy depends entirely on a hunter's consistency in establishing mutual respect with the game he is pursuing. Boasting of one's ability and wasting meat are serious breaches of etiquette that will disturb one's relationship with game and discourage animals from being killed. Respect is shown through a patient attitude toward the hunt and proper handling of game that has been taken. The strength of these attitudes is described by a hunter in Chisasibi:

> Sometimes a hunter is unintentionally disrespectful to animals…. My brother was trapping otter. He had left his trap in the water a bit too long, normally [sic], one checks traps quite often. There was an otter in the trap, but it had been in the water too long. The fur was coming off. My brother was really worried: he had caused the fur to spoil, and knew that this was a crime against the animals. He said the otter would retaliate for this by making itself unavail-

able. He thought it would take perhaps three years before the otter would decide to come back to his trap again (Cree Trappers Association, 1989: 21–22).

The uncertainty surrounding human relationships with animals, the sometimes inscrutable offenses that can make game unavailable even to the most accomplished hunter, are an incentive to use rituals, divination, charms, and dream revelations to predict animal behavior and improve hunting success. The most common actions performed to enhance productivity of the hunt involve the handling of animal carcasses. Skulls and antlers of game animals are hung in trees as gestures of respect, and as requests to the animal that it continue offering itself to hunters. Black bears continue to be regarded as the most spiritually powerful animal, capable of influencing the outcomes of all hunting efforts; special care is made to ensure proper handling of the carcass: "A black bear is brought into camp. Hunters sit in a circle, with the bear in the middle. Someone smokes a pipe beside the bear and makes a gesture of offering the pipe to the bear. Or a piece of tobacco is placed in the bear's mouth as an offering. Once the bear is skinned, a chunk of the meat is thrown into the fire" (Cree Trappers Association, 1989: 31). Respectful handling of the skull is also important. The correct procedure is observed when the bear's jawbone is tied to the skull before being hung in a tree. I once saw an elder sharply scold a teenager who had placed a bear skull on the ground while distractedly trying to fit the jawbone. His action, it seemed, was not befitting an animal of such importance.

The most common form of divination, used to predict the arrival of visitors or the location of animals, is scapulimancy—reading signs in a flat bone, usually a shoulder blade, that has been charred and cracked by fire. The distribution of bush radios to remote camps in the early 1980s may have reduced the need to predict the arrival of planes to the camp, but the practice continues for interpreting the activity of game and fortunes of the hunt. Tanner (1979: 118–119) describes porcupine scapulars as having special importance, but the shoulder blades of caribou, rabbit, and even the breastbones of birds are also used. The Cree Trappers Association of Chisasibi provides a simple guide for the interpretation of charred bones: "One puts the shoulder blade in the fire. The fire will slowly start to burn through the bone. The first spot that appears on the bone is your camp. The other spots that begin to appear on the bone indicate game and visitors to the camp. The way the burn travels on the bone gives clues regarding distance and direction of movement" (1989: 24–25). Tanner (1979: 119) describes charred bones being shown around the camp and widely discussed before any decision is made about what they reveal. Particular individuals are recognized as having a knack for bringing out subtleties of interpretation and having more reliability in their forecasts than others.

Married couples often pay particular attention to the woman's dreams, which are thought to be directly tied to her husband's chances of bringing home game. Metaphoric symbolism is usually found to have some connection with hunting and trapping activity in the future, sometimes in a direct way, such as a dream about the spiritually powerful bear, or more indirectly, as in dreams about animals in human form. There is also, as Brightman reports, a tendency towards deliberateness in the dreaming process: "Crees say that they attempt to dream about specific objects of desire, maintain consciousness during the transition into sleep, recognize when they are dreaming, and act volitionally within dreams whether or not the dream is one they understand themselves to have cultivated" (1993: 99). In dreaming, as in some other spiritual activities relating to hunting, there is no sharp boundary between divination and ritual, prediction and control. Volitional dreaming is done to improve one's success, while other dreams might be understood to say something about the future. Similarly, cracking a bear's knuckles to see whether or not it is withholding game from the hunter is both a way to acquire knowledge, and a release from the power of the bear. Control and insight in spiritual relationships with animals are important aspects of the forest lifestyle that has relied on success in hunting, trapping, and fishing for survival and prosperity.

The spiritual forces of the forest are not limited to the creatures that dwell there. Rocks, trees, features of the landscape—all can have a special significance that stands out in the course of daily activities. For example, as Robbie Matthew, Sr. explained, water can sometimes have both curative and meditative values:

> This river here [the La Grande] was once a mighty river, a very powerful river. [The place] where the rapids used to start from, that water was so powerful that you could cure yourself with it.... Hydro wants to get that power, use it in a different way; but we, as indigenous people, have always respected that power in the water.... When you want to go on the land, connect yourself with the rapids, the fresh water, not the water that you take from the reservoir; its not going to give you any effects at all. But if you go off the reservoir and into my territory, there's a lot of rapids there. And if you want to cure yourself with the water, go there, take some, and boil yourself some tea. Then you will notice the texture, the taste, because its powerful. I usually go there during my time in the bush. I go there just to watch the rapids.

For those who are overwhelmed by the pace of life and changes taking place in the communities, the forest can provide an important respite.

The realm of spiritual understanding in the forest is different from that provided by the formal Churches of the communities, but this does not mean that Christianity is seen to be incompatible with forest life. While relationships with animals can be seen to determine hunting success, the metaphysical source of human and animal life for committed Christians is still the one Provider. Almost universally, hunting does not take place on Sundays. Men do not fire guns on the Sabbath, nor set new traps or nets. Women similarly do not take on projects such as chopping wood or gathering spruce boughs (Cree Trappers Association, 1989: 39). At the same time, however, spiritual behavior is widely recognized as different in the forest. "Elders have two sets of knowledge," a young man from Chisasibi pointed out to me, "the intimate knowledge they have from the bush setting...and the reflections they get from the Church." Frank Speck observed the same thing in the 1920s, writing in the condescending style characteristic of his times, when he saw that hunters who were scrupulous in their Christian observance in settlements with missions changed their behavior in the isolation of the forest: "When the hunters have returned to the interior, they are again under the thrall of the spiritual forces of the forest; and except for some acquired rules of conduct, and an attempt, always too vague for their theological comprehension, to imitate the services of the far-off "prayer-house," their orthodoxy becomes an exotic memory (Speck, 1977: 20–21). The success of missions in Cree communities did not fully compromise the beliefs and practices of forest spirituality which sees animals as possessing sacred power, controlling the outcome of human activities, and the forces of the natural world having restorative and curative powers.

HEALING

Another important aspect of Cree attachment to the land is the indigenous system of healing, which uses products of the forest to effect cures for a wide variety of ailments. The holistic approach of Cree healing involves not only the inseparable nature of body and spirit but also an intimate connection between man and the natural world. The Cree word *"miyupimaatisiiun,"* best translated as 'being alive well' or 'in a good condition of life,' was explained by an elder in Chisasibi as an ability to lead an active life in the forest, to follow the Cree way of life. This notion of health implies not only physical vigor and spiritual well-being, but extends to the individual's social and natural environments (Lavallée, 1991: 4). Another elder in Chisasibi, put it this way: "The term *miyupimaatisiiun* means constantly moving, exercising, doing things. Because when you're moving there's no stress.... [Out on the land] you would have no ailment because there's no time for that. You're always on the move.... Your mind is doing different things every day."[11]

The perception of active participation in the forest way of life as the essential criterion of health has its counterpart in

---

11. From an interview in Chisasibi, October 10, 1995, translated from Cree by Annie House.

the use of the forest as a strategy in healing. Emotional disturbances that occurred in the newly centralized village of Mistassini in the 1940s and 1950s, as former chief Henry Mianscum recalls, were sometimes informally treated through a reintegration of the patient in the hunting activity of remote camps. "[The elders] recommended a therapy...using their basic cultural knowledge of what life in the bush is all about. You get serenity. You get peace." This kind of healing power of the forest is a resource that continues to be used: "A lot of people can tell you, if they are under great stress...the only way they can see themselves being cured is going into the bush."

Another important aspect of Cree medicine is the spiritual nature of the healing process. This is most apparent in the way an elder from Chisasibi summarizes the power once controlled by shamans:

> Probably [shamans] could help anything, help anybody.... They could cure any disease. Even they could raise anybody from the dead. [But] the native people here in Chisasibi lost their own power...because they were not allowed to perform any rituals or traditional ceremonies. They lost it because the Church itself, the minister, [was] telling them "this is evil, this is wrong, what you're doing."

Even herbal healing is sometimes seen to depend for its success on the spiritual attitude of healer and patient. Gathering medicinal plants was one of the activities in which an attitude of spiritual humility was important: "When using natural medicine you always have to show respect to the Creator by dressing [properly] and asking for the things you'll be taking. After the herbs are gathered, you in return have to put something back. The way this was done was an offering of tobacco to the Creator. Show your thanks. Every living thing has the power to heal if you have faith and know how to use [medicine] and ask for it."[12] For some healers, prayer was an essential part of healing.

---

12. The speaker of this radio narrative and her village of origin were not identified.

I'll be talking about my great-grandchild. She was plagued with impetigo, and she used to have a strong reaction to insect bites. And one day they asked me to try the Native medicine on her. So I used a muskrat skin. First I asked for some dry tamarack wood.... I had to put the wood in the fire for it to work. And I started to pray to the Creator to be with me during the healing. There is a prayer that is said while the wood is put into the fire. Later I asked for a young tree to be brought to me with all the branches snipped off. And I put the head of the muskrat skin on it and put it in the fire. Then I started asking the grandfather spirit to help this child: "take away the impetigo from this child." Have faith in the medicine that is used. It'll work if you have faith. So I rubbed the medicine all over her face and arms.... Ever since I put the medicine on her, she's not been plagued with it anymore. And she never has reactions to insect bites either.[13]

The prayers that were used in gathering and applying the medicine for this patient—fat burned from the head of a freshly killed muskrat—were just as important as the medicine itself.

Although shamans were described as an important resource for healing and divination, especially during the summer months when people from widely scattered camps congregated in settlements, narratives of Cree healing situate the family as by far the most important resource in handling health-related emergencies. Despite the difficulties involved in observing family healing activity, Kleinman (1980: 306–307) posits some of its essential features as involving continuous, informal transactions, and open discussions of culturally shared knowledge. With respect to the Cree we can add that family-based healing in the forest setting is associated with the respect (*chistaiitimuun*) and informal leadership roles bestowed on knowledgeable elders. This is illustrated by a description of the treatment of a broken leg.

---

13. Excerpt from a radio narrative recorded in Chisasibi.

> My father said the [boy's] sled hit a tree breaking
> his leg. The people were very worried and fright-
> ened. His bone was sticking out off [*sic*] his thigh.
> His bone was completely broken.
> "I wonder what would have happened to that
> boy if I was not here," my father said. My father
> gripped the leg, trying to reconstruct before the boy
> felt pain. The bone crackled while my father did
> this. He wrapped it tightly so the leg wouldn't
> move. My father was like a great medicine trying to
> straighten and reconstruct the boy's leg (*The Nation*,
> 1995a: 11).

Healers with many years of experience in forest life were
relied upon to save lives in a setting that combined remoteness from human settlement with numerous routine
hazards. Elders were the repositories of both practical
knowledge and spiritual power which combined to give
them a heroic quality, "like great medicine."

Cree attachment to the land is not based upon a desire
for material gain. Nor is it based primarily upon goals of
community improvement through industrial exploitation of
natural resources in competition with non-native corpora-
tions, even in communities whose band councils sponsor
Cree-owned logging operations.[14] Rather, it is grounded in a
perception of the importance of maintaining forest life. This
is seen to provide a sense of continuity with the practices of
ancestors and, for some elders, fulfilling the time-honored
promise of maintaining the land intact for future generations. In the days of the ancestors, this promise was honored
by hunters though developing a close spiritual relationship

---

14. The most prominent example of Cree-owned resource extraction is the
    partnership between Waswanipi's Mishtuk Corporation and Domtar
    Inc. to log on and off Waswanipi's lands. Cree tallymen were required
    to give their authorization for the logging operation to go ahead and
    the project was associated with careful environmental monitoring.
    Waswanipi Chief John Kitchen defended the controversial operation
    saying, "We've been a model for other forestry operations. In the office
    we have a satellite photo of the area that shows the difference between
    Mishtuk's operations and the other companies. There's a huge
    difference" (*The Nation* 1996b: 7).

with animals in order to maintain a productive harvest; with the advent of the fur trade, formal game management procedures, especially quotas on the beaver harvest, were required by law; and in recent decades, a Cree political leadership, acting in response to the threats of large-scale development and provincial/federal government realignment, has added yet another dimension to the hunters' responsibilities as stewards of the land.

The incentive to defend forest life is also grounded in a wide recognition of the potential of the land to heal. The abilities of many hunters to use the Cree system of medicine for simple remedies continues to be part of the daily life in the camps. There are also some elders with more sophisticated knowledge of 'traditional' healing, specialists who use their medicines with a recognition of the power inherent in products of the forest and other spiritual forces that encourage healing.

A more general improvement in health can also take place through the calming influence of forest life which can radically change the demeanors of individuals and improve communication between family members and those from different generations. This understanding of the importance of forest life has only emerged in contrast to the discomfort and apathy felt by many in rapidly changing communities and urban centers. A social worker in Chisasibi noted a common pattern among her clients: "A lot of the people I see…seem to exist on a daily basis. They don't have any goals. They don't have any aspirations." Even those with regular employment can find life in the community hard to adjust to: "a lot of us have problems dealing with the lifestyle here because you're living from Monday to Friday. You're working in the office…the way the white man lives." Finding enough time to go out on the land is difficult when faced with the demands of formal employment. But for those who do, the experience is often described as part of a healing process. "[When] I knew I was not going in the right direction, I would correct myself, go out there [in the bush] and find myself."

Forest life today can be seen as one side of a dual lifestyle in which the bush camps and villages require distinct forms of leadership, technologies, and practical skills of their inhabitants. Whether the realms of forest and village can at some point intersect to create a broad base of cultural strength or tend more often to divide themselves into distinct and incompatible lifeways is an issue that can only be addressed once we have outlined the ways that settled villages and formal institutions have gained importance in the James Bay region.

3

The Origins of a Dual Lifestyle

The term "person" means an individual other than an Indian...
Government of Canada,
Indian Act of 1880, Section 12.

Even a drive-through tour of a road accessible Cree community can reveal some of the ways that the forest and village intersect. Fishing nets are hung out to bleach in the sun to eliminate scents that warn fish away. Skulls and antlers, tokens of respect to hunted animals, are sometimes visible hanging from back-yard trees or the siding of sheds and houses. Boys, encouraged to practice hunting, can occasionally be glimpsed stalking through the brush at the edge of the village, trying their aim on small birds or stray chipmunks with slingshots that are usually home-made from forked willow branches and surgical tubing or strips from rubber gaskets taken from discarded heavy machinery. Sometimes, especially in the coastal communities, they can be seen practicing goose hunting by throwing stones at a moving target, by preference a 'frisbee', or making goose calls that demand the kind of range from a middle- to high-octave that only pre-pubescent children seem to be able to properly master. These are all signs of the perpetuation of a hunting-way of life.

In the bush camps themselves the other side of this inter-penetration of forest and village is perhaps more easily visible. Here, motorized means of transport are in almost daily use. Four-wheelers, snowmobiles, and heavy 'freighter' canoes and outboard motors, show a more than recreational interest in securing transport to remote wilderness. Without them, movement between the camps and communities would hampered, sometimes impossible, and short stays in the camps would not be possible for those who work or attend school in the communities. Once there, chain saws, bush radios, and well-stocked medical kits, are examples of more or less permanent camp technology relied upon in different ways to improve the quality of life: saving labor, facilitating contact with other camps and with communities, and maintaining or restoring health.

Despite these technological advantages, not everyone can live comfortably as contributing members of a camp. Trapping, fishing, hunting, and maintaining a camp are skills that require long experience to develop an expertise. Travel in the wilderness can be very dangerous when the landscape is unfamiliar or when an individual alone is unable to judge the safety of ice, which can vary enormously depending not only on the air temperature, but also water currents, the depth of a lake, the insulating effect of a blanket of snow, or the weight of a load being carried on one's back. Weather conditions can shift dramatically, leading to disorientation and exposure. Technology by itself cannot eliminate many of the hazards of life in the forest nor bring a person to function productively within it. A childhood spent attending school in the town is enough to make life in the traditional economy difficult and sometimes unattainable—the number of years of experience during the formative period of youth seem to be an important part of the background of those functioning in the traditional economy.

The existence of a dual lifestyle is therefore nothing short of miraculous, given the kinds of pressures that have been exerted to 'develop' the wilderness and to settle more people permanently in villages. By outlining the history of these pressures, and the Cree responses to them, we can better understand present social patterns and political contests. The fur trade in the nineteenth century is the logical place to begin a description of pressures toward sedentarization and the origins of the dual lifestyle, since it marked the beginning of social arrangements that encouraged regular affiliation of Cree families with designated trading posts and settlement in one area during the inactive summer months. The fur trade, as I will demonstrate, was not a significant threat to the forest lifestyle; nor was it characterized, as some have assumed, by European domination and native victimization, but more by a selective, critical approach on the part of Cree hunters to key features of European technology and culture.

More permanent changes were made by efforts to intentionally alter cultural patterns, through the combined influence of Anglican missions, formal medicine, and residential education. In different ways, missions, medicine, and schools aimed to assimilate native people into Euro-Canadian society with little regard for the cultural importance of the forest lifestyle. Permanent communities were eventually built up around missionary and government institutions, increasingly widening the distance between forest and village. But not all of the missionary and government efforts to assimilate native people resulted in cultural destruction. While residential school programs distanced many children from experience on the land and were for some psychologically traumatic, they also eventually produced an articulate bicultural leadership that became central to the negotiation and implementation of regional autonomy and protection of the forest lifestyle. The signs of hunting and fishing activities visible in the Cree communities today are largely outcomes of political contests and compromises between government and a new, formally educated native leadership.

THE FUR TRADE

From the first period of contact between natives and immigrants in the New World, the fur trade was to become a focus of mercantile interests. Beaver pelts, with longer guard hairs removed to expose only the wool or felt, was an extremely popular and lucrative trade item from the seventeenth to nineteenth centuries. Beaver felt was used extensively in European hat manufacture, acting as an immediately recognizable marker of social status. North America became the almost exclusive source of beaver pelt for several reasons. European beaver populations had, by the seventeenth century, already been reduced to near extinction, making the new continent a more productive source. The processing of pelts in North America was also superior. The natural way to remove guard hairs, by wearing the fur next to the skin for a season or two, was used by native trappers to produce a thick, glossy, superior-quality pelt that could not be imitated by other means. Above all, the fur trade in North America, despite the expense and hardship of transatlantic travel, was more profitable than existing trade markets in Europe. Fur traders could exchange ordinary items of European manufacture—use items such as kettles, knives, axes, firearms, powder and ammunition, decorative objects such as beads and copper, consumable goods such as flour, sugar, tobacco, and alcohol—for beaver and other furs sold in European markets as luxury items. The relative value of the items exchanged provided North American fur traders with a potential for huge profits.[1]

It was the ever-present desire on the part of the Hudson's Bay Company to increase its profits that encouraged trends toward Cree settlement around trading posts. The absorption by the Hudson's Bay Company of its only significant rival in the James Bay region, the North West Company, in 1821 prompted a realignment of the distribution of trading posts and an expansion eastward to regions that were more accessible to inland camps. At the same time the Hudson's Bay Company initiated an accounting system that discouraged trappers from taking credit at more than one post. Hunters using other posts still had their furs provisionally accepted, but transactions were credited to the 'home' post to which they were assigned. And, as Francis and Morantz

---

1. For a general discussion of the North American fur trade see Wolf, 1982: ch. 6.

write, "Indians who 'wandered' were mistrusted by the company officers for being suspicious characters" (1983: 123). The net effect was to encourage families to settle around one particular post in the summer months. "Whatever the bureaucratic benefits to the company, the effect on the Indians was to restrict their traditional freedom of movement.... [T]he families, who maintained themselves by fishing, often settled close to the posts...and in this way the posts acquired a permanent summertime population of Indians" (Francis and Morantz, 1983: 123). This early movement in the direction of permanent settlements was, however, not far-reaching in its overall impact on the Cree way of life. During the summer months, hunting families were temporarily more centralized and their mobility in relation to trading posts more restricted, but subsistence remained firmly anchored to the activities of the forest. Hunters also seem to have easily handled the cultural impact of the presence of traders and the authority structure of the trading company. The families that traded at Fort Rupert (today called Waskaganish) in the nineteenth and early twentieth centuries would pause at a specially designated spot before entering the trading post with their furs. A quiet bend in a creek, today referred to as 'Dress-Up Creek', was used as a place to wash up, take clothes out of caches, and dress in a style considered more pleasing to the Europeans in the post (MacGregor, 1990: 80). With undiminished attachment to hunting and trapping, the Crees were easily able to master the movement from forest to settlement, and interpret and act upon the expectations of non-natives attempting to exert profit-motivated authority.

MISSIONS, MEDICINE, AND RESIDENTIAL EDUCATION

Although trading posts were instrumental in creating the first permanent settlements in Cree territory, they were not responsible for any significant discontinuity in the forest lifestyle. One possible exception to this was the federal government's imposition of beaver quotas in the 1930s in response to a sharp decline in the beaver population. This was caused mainly by the intrusion of non-native trappers onto Cree territory, a development which led in turn to over harvesting by Cree trappers in competition with outsiders who were unaccountable to the informal Cree system of game regulation. In some regions, this crisis corresponded with a period of starvation on the traplines. With the eventual restoration of the beaver and restriction of the activities of non-native trappers, fur-trading relations again returned to a situation in which Cree hunters exercised *de facto* authority over their traplines (Scott, 1988).

More widespread and portentous changes to Cree culture took place through the influence of missionary activity in the James Bay region, the main purpose of which was to 'assimilate' the Indians, to teach them the important lessons and rituals of Christianity in order to save their souls and ease their inevitable transition into civilized society. This objective was put into practice through three institutions: churches, clinics, and schools. Initially, the programs associated with religion, medicine, and education were combined in small-scale missionary efforts, but eventually each was developed within a distinct institutional framework. Together, these institutions of acculturation combined to alter (some might prefer the word 'diversify') Cree systems of belief, creating a greater social and cultural distance between forest and village.

The first exposure the Cree people of the James Bay had with Christianity, 'European' medicine, and literacy did not come through missions but through the personnel of the Hudson's Bay Company. The principal posts, which in the James Bay would only have included Moose Factory in Ontario, maintained 'surgeons' until they were replaced by government doctors who began annual visits with treaty delegations at the end of the nineteenth century. Rudiments of Christianity, without the apparatus of formal education, were sometimes communicated by Hudson's Bay Company managers and, with similar amateurism, medical services were offered by them. Alan Nicholson, the Post Manager at Rupert's House (now Waskaganish) at the turn of the century, is described in a fur trader's autobiography as the principal healer of the community: "[He] had quite a reputation as an amateur practitioner, and many an Indian, and not a few white people too, had him to thank for timely medical aid. He had several medical books which he studied from time to time, and of course experience and practice in catering to Indian ailments led to increased proficiency" (J. Anderson, 1961: 43).

A systematic effort to educate and convert the residents of the James Bay did not exist until the company's charter was renewed in 1837 with a new stipulation that it improve the Indians' spiritual condition (Long, 1986: 314). In 1840 the Wesleyan Methodist missionary, George Barnley, was the first to receive funding and be granted passage on HBC ships for the purpose of meeting this perceived need. His missionary circuit stretched from Great Whale River on the eastern side of Hudson Bay, to the settlement of Albany on the western shore of James Bay. He was largely frustrated in his efforts at conversion, often lamenting in his letters and journal entries about the poor retentive capacities of native intellects and their supposed inability to comprehend even the most basic of Christian principles (Long, 1986). Complaints by early missionaries also extended to Cree attitudes toward the medicine dispensed as part of their charitable work. Edwin Watkins, who succeeded Barnley in 1851 under the banner of the Church Mission Society, felt that native taciturnity led them to take his acts of kindness for granted. The recipients considered "all acts of kindness, & all gifts, whether of food, clothing or medicine as a matter of course…[although they] felt little need for assistance for the soul…they readily applied for help for the *body*" (Long, 1985: 94).

Early missionaries should not perhaps have been surprised at being solicited for medical aid, given the devastating impact of epidemics caused by pathogens of European origin that periodically swept through native communities and sometimes resulted in more than a fifty percent mortality rate. A Church Mission Society (CMS) biography of Bishop Horden describes his activities when an epidemic of influenza almost wiped out the entire native population of Albany in 1884: "He was, compared with [the Indians], in health and full of the bright, cheerful faith which they had seen him show in times of hardship before. He was here, there, and everywhere amongst them, distributing medicine and food; comforting the dying, burying the dead, consoling the bereaved; setting the convalescent to such tasks as they were fit for" (Buckland, 1895: 101).

In the minds of some Cree elders there is an inextricable link between early missionary activity and disease. As Willis writes in her autobiography of childhood in Fort George, "[my great grandmother] told me…of how the early missionaries, after proving their superiority by making good their threats of strange illnesses—smallpox, TB, etc.—and death if the Indians did not accept the white man's God, had gradually converted everyone to Christianity…. She blamed all illnesses, especially mine, on lack of faith" (Willis, 1973: 7).

In assessing the social impact of this confluence of epidemics and conversion efforts it is easy to assume that the devastation wrought by epidemics would affect both spiritual and productive activities, that widespread suffering would bring into doubt the spiritual and healing practices intended to provide protection and healing. Trigger, considering the impact of epidemics among the Huron of the seventeenth century, does not consider the delegitimation of spiritual beliefs and practices to have been a significant result of epidemics. Rather, the abrupt loss of a large number of knowledgeable elders had the most significant consequences because of an interruption in the transmission of cultural knowledge. "Traditional religious lore tended to be a prerogative of the elderly, and many must have died before they could transmit what they knew to their heirs. The loss of such a broad spectrum of knowledge must have made the Hurons economically still more reliant on the French and less able at a theological level to resist the attacks of the Jesuits" (Trigger, 1985: 250). A similar argument could probably be made for the Cree, but in this case the impact of disease on cultural continuity was probably less significant than among the Huron. The wide dispersal of the population in hunting territories reduced the general demographic impact of epidemics. Healing by ritual specialists was active in Cree society well past the time when pathogens of European origin were most destructive of lives and culture.

At the same time that epidemics were raging through native settlements, missionaries strove to eliminate native curing practices that, from their point of view, were suspect. When Reverend Anderson, the Bishop of Rupert's Land, made a tour of the western James Bay region in 1852, he recorded in his journal an encounter with a Cree elder whom he judged to be "sensible and rather superior" because of his profession of Christianity. Anderson expressed concern, however, about the spiritual influence of herbal healing: "He is very unwilling… to give up his medicinal art, which, he says, consists only in the knowledge of roots, not in anything of charms or conjuration. If we could believe his statement we might be satisfied; but it is very difficult to separate the things entirely, and to effect an actual divorce between the two offices" (D. Anderson, 1854: 53).

'Conjuring', or shamanism (*miitaaun*) was the most significant indigenous rival to Christianity and all activities

The old Anglican Church and Cemetery, Fort George Island.

even remotely associated with it were deemed suspect. When 'Reindeer' Walton began his tenure as a CMS missionary in Great Whale in 1892, his efforts were directed toward the elimination of shamanism. Decades of missionary activity in the region, and a receptiveness among the Cree to new forms of religious expression, gave him the spiritual authority to introduce sweeping changes to indigenous ritual and healing practices. Walton's knowledge of Cree language and culture gave him the insight to direct his conversion effort toward the *miitaau*, shamans, who were initially able to combine Christianity with indigenous roles to enhance their local spiritual influence. In some cases, as Bishop Lawrence reported to me, shamans substituted their indigenous role for the position of 'catechist' or 'lay reader'. "The Church Missionary Society seems to have used the role of catechist a lot.... everywhere they went it seems they would raise up local leaders and have them first as teachers of the faith before they were ordained."

Eventually, Walton was able to categorically ban some practices seen by him to be anti-Christian. The use of the drum by shamans in curing and by hunters in singing remembrances of their pursuit of game, was perceived to be particularly offensive. The most common use of the drum was an individual 'performance' as the instrument, suspended by a string from the roof of the lodge, was held lightly in the hunter's lap and used to accompany repeated stanzas telling about the highlights of activity on the land. But as Bishop Lawrence explained, Walton saw the drum as being more than a musical instrument, "It was used quite deliberately to work people into frenzies. I think in his view it was an instrument of the devil."

Closely associated with shamanic healing, and equally excoriated by missionaries, was the shaking tent, a setting in which individuals could contact the spirit world for guidance and knowledge of the future with shamans acting as mediums. A small, conical tent with enough room for only one person was erected with poles driven firmly into the ground. The shaman would enter and, if all went well, would soon begin a dialogue with the spirits. Spectators would sometimes see the tent sway wildly and hear voices and animal noises as the shaman directed his questions to the spirit world. As one narrator from Chisasibi put it, "It acted like the phone system, but no wires were needed.... The spirits were the life-lines of the shaking tent."[2] A description of shaking tent seances from a trader in Mistassini in 1911 stresses the emotional atmosphere generated by the hidden activities of shamans:

> The conjurer, or medicine man, begins to beat on the drum and very soon the whole tent village is electrified. The actual conjuring is hidden from view inside the conjurer's tent, and sometimes is carried on for a hour or more...in surroundings like these—in any vast vacant quiet—the senses play uncommonly queer tricks with their possessor. The very air, in its autumn crispness, seems to be astir with the sounds and shapes on the edge of revelation (J. Anderson, 1961: 101).

In their programs of cultural reform, missionaries did not distinguish between shaking tents and sweat lodges, both associated with visionary experiences. As Bruchac writes, "Sweat bathing was often described [by Europeans] as an ignorant, and unhealthy and a savage custom...[and] the association of the sweat bath with ceremony contributed to the sweat bath being labeled as yet another instrument of the devil" (1993: 25). Among the Cree, the practice of throwing water on red-hot stones in the central pit of a dome-shaped tent was used for curing a wide variety of ailments, including tuberculosis, pneumonia and influenza. When available, it provided an effective emergency treatment for hypothermia. It was also, as one narrator recalled, used to help people with mental illness:

> I remember my wife being healed of mental stress. It was bad at that time because she couldn't eat. All she was doing was throwing up. That's how she was. What [we] did was to have a [session in] a

---

2. Excerpt from a radio narrative recorded in Chisasibi.

sweat lodge. My father told me about this. He told us both to go in the sweat lodge. We didn't put any clothing on. We were really in a sweat when we were in there. We stayed in there for three hours. Once we were out, we just wiped ourselves with a towel…We had to be really careful that we didn't cool of instantly after the sweat. Just gradually. And after having done the sweat we noticed she was improving. She started feeling well.[3]

The cultural reform of missionaries was to uproot a range of healing practices seen to be at odds with Christian teachings and the goals of evangelism.

It is important to stress that native people were not merely passive recipients of missionary persuasion. Some scholars argue that the combined forces of European contact did not lead to the destruction of essential features of native culture. In the use of tools and technology, in particular, European innovations were incorporated "devoid of their European ideological content and assigned Indian meanings" (Thistle, 1986: 35). Morantz argues for the cultural autonomy of the Cree, especially in terms of the technology, strategies, and rituals of hunting which she sees as natural continuations of ancient activities (Morantz, 1978: 122). Even in more direct attempts to change native culture, such as in the educational activities, 'social action', and evangelization of missions, the impact can be seen to result more in adjustment than destruction.

In some ways, the Cree response to evangelism bears out the adjustment approach to the social impact of early missions. Spiritual leaders who converted to Christianity may only have changed the superficial aspects of their role while retaining or even enhancing the substance of their positions and strategies of leadership. Moreover, Walton was frustrated by the persistence of some spiritual ideas and practices that resisted influence from Christian teachings and his own

---

3. Excerpt from a radio narrative recorded in Mistissini.

personal and formidable powers of persuasion. One of these was the venerations of bears:

> They have numerous superstitious ideas concerning him & it will take many years of teaching to get them out of some. Some think he does not sleep all the winter, but simply retires to meditate. It is a very common belief amongst them that he understands when they speak to him, & some believe he has a soul like a man. I have gathered the Indians together & spoken very plainly about these foolish ideas & one old man was perfectly convinced, but I am afraid that it will be a very long time before many of their ideas will be given up (Long, 1985: 110)

Even today, apocryphal stories and jokes about misunderstandings, doubts, and subtle protest from Walton's congregation circulate in Chisasibi, more than seventy years after the events are said to have taken place, providing another example of resistance to missionary activity.

Yet in Chisasibi those who reject the Church and voice opposition to the destructive practices of Christianity do not normally reject the faith as a whole. The way that religion was taught and what is perceived as the hypocrisy and intolerance of some of its missionaries are understood to have been damaging to Cree society. But the teachings of Christianity itself are seen as valuable in themselves and consistent with Cree traditions. In a document entitled 'Dominant Cultures Influence on the Cree way of Life', the authors had this to say about Chisasibi's missionary legacy:

> Listening to the knowledge and wisdom of the elders, native peoples understood, adapted the new religious teachings, because they interwove their own spiritual beliefs deriving from the Cree cultural background. In fact the Cree people were already practicing values such as respect, sharing love, kinship, etc.... which are also promoted in the Bible. The missionaries did not practice what they were preaching.... Instead they preached against the native social practices, ceremonies and spiritual beliefs,

as remembered by many elders" (Herodier, Duff, and Pash, 1992: 3).

Cree social critics of non-native society therefore accept many of the values of Christianity but the remembered history of missionary activity has left questions about the manner in which formal religion was taught and put into practice.

Christian missions in the James Bay region were intolerant of some important aspects of Cree healing and spirituality. Missionary efforts, seeking not just to evangelize but also to civilize and 'improve' native society, led to replacement of indigenous healing practices with 'proper' medicine, replacement of 'conjuring' with the ironically compatible virtues of 'faith' and 'science'. As Bishop Lawrence explained, the early practice of the Church Mission Society was to combine evangelism, education, and medicine: "They didn't just devote themselves to evangelism, but they established schools, they set up…health centers…It was a social action ministry as well as an evangelistic ministry."

Social action was also the platform of the Catholic missionary presence in Fort George which began in the 1920s, long after the Anglican Church had become fully established. It was, in fact, owing to their disadvantaged position in interdenominational competition, that the Catholics stressed services before evangelism and came to have a central place in the technological development and institutionalization of medicine in the community of Fort George.

Père Boisseau, who began his tenure in Fort George in the 1920s, practiced medicine in a personal way similar to the approach of his predecessors from other denominations. As Père Alain described it to me, Boisseau "Helped these people a great deal with the little bit of knowledge that he had and the little bit of medicine he had. But [among people who have] nothing at all, a little bit seems like a lot." Sensing both urgent medical and educational needs in Fort George, Boisseau sought funds for the expansion of mission services. He died in 1929, having obtained these resources, but before the school and clinic were built. In 1930, the Catholic school and clinic were constructed and four *sœurs grises*, 'grey sisters', arrived to practice education and healing. The clinic, with only three beds, could admit only the very ill, while others were treated as out-patients. The school was initially even less successful, having only one student who was, in addition to educational services, being treated for chronic illness. This number was to increase to five by the mid-1940s with the enrollment of students from other settlements on both sides of the bay. As Willis recalls in her account of growing up in Fort George, "Our parents were too terrified of the constant threats of eternal hell and damnation to send their children to the Catholic school" (Willis, 1973: 26).

Unlike its moderately successful medical facility, the Catholic day-school was unable to compete with its Anglican counterpart, the St. Phillip's Indian and Eskimo Anglican Residential School, which opened its doors in 1947 with funding from the Indian Affairs branch of the Department of Citizenship and Immigration. The forty-eight students who made up the entering class ranged in age from five to sixteen. Aside from two months in the summer and three-hour visits on Saturdays, even those with immediate relatives in the village were required to reside in the school. It was a closed setting intended to teach native children the language, values, and cultural heritage of Euro-Canadian society while at the same time distancing them from their 'pagan' ancestry. Jane Willis, in her autobiography of residential education, recalls an almost total emphasis on religious curriculum. In a speech to incoming students, the Anglican minister made it very clear that their purpose in staying in the school was to learn Christianity: "[T]he most important reason why you are here is to learn all about God and His son, Jesus Christ. Since your ancestors were heathens, you must try harder than other people to get into the kingdom of God" (Willis, 1973: 5). But there was to be more than just Christian teachings. In addition to religious instruction students experienced an occasional secular curriculum, albeit one that was often completely alien to life on the Island, including a two-week session in the grade one class devoted to reading traffic signals and other rules of the road, remembered as a bizarre experience for students on a remote island crisscrossed only with foot trails (Willis, 1973: 35).

The curriculum was not the only alienating aspect of residential school. Native students were taught in no uncertain terms that learning Christianity meant leaving behind 'pagan,' 'savage' ancestors. The way of life even of close family members was described a barbaric, superstitious, and unhygienic. As one former student of St. Phillip's remembers, "Growing up in school, you learn to behave yourself and leave your tradition behind. That's the way I was taught to become a Christian." The first step to closing the door on this life of wayward ignorance was to be isolated in the school environment and systematically stripped of all identification with the past. For new students this meant changing outward forms of identification: haircuts, delousing, and the assignment of numbers were part of their initial school experience. Perhaps even more traumatic was a total prohibition of the Cree language, with English being the only accepted medium of communication. This was a rule that most refused to follow. Cree was still used in the absence of staff members, while English was used in the classroom; and the error of accidentally slipping into Cree in the wrong situation usually resulted in a strapping.

In terms of direct implications for Cree life on the land, residential education involved a physical removal from the knowledge and experience of the forest. Children raised in a 'total institution' did not acquire many of the skills associated with life in the bush. A hunter in Chisasibi told me, "A lot of people, especially the ones that have been to school, have a hard time going back [to the bush] because it's hard to be [there] unless you're very skilled." All adults living in the forest possess a large reserve of knowledge about the behavior of a wide variety of game animals, the techniques used in catching them, the best climate and conditions for pursuing particular species, and techniques for staying safe and comfortable in all weather. Those skilled in the forest lifestyle sometimes point out that this knowledge takes a great deal of experience to acquire thoroughly and is easily lost if close contact with the environment is not maintained.

[A] young man returned to his community after being away for several years at the residential school.

That fall he went into the bush to trap with his father. The camp was in an area known to him. His father sent him to check the traps. He made it to the
traps without any difficulty but on the way back, he
got disoriented and he was completely lost. The old
man, missing him, went to look for him. He called
him but had no luck. He went to the traps, but the
young man was not there. It was getting late so they
called off the search that day. The following day,
they found him. He had spent the night under a
clump of trees which served him as a sort of shelter.
He had not even built a fire; that is, he had been
completely helpless. On a really cold day, he would
not have survived. In the old days, a 16-year-old
would have been considered an adult in terms of
how he handled himself in the bush (Cree Trappers
Association, 1989: 58).

Students also did not have many experiences of being treated by a family member who used traditional medicine
resources. Ideas of etiology, prevention, and treatment were
now introduced in the classroom.

As the missions became more successful and more committed to social programs, formal institutions were developed as key resources in the dissemination of spiritual and
medical ideas and practices. In Fort George, boarding
schools and clinics were used by competing Anglican and
Catholic denominations to change or reinforce religious,
economic, and health-related behavior. The socializing
power of these institutions, however, was not lost on federal
authorities who were to act upon a renewed commitment to
bring native people into the mainstream of Canadian society
by taking a more active responsibility for Indian health care,
education, and political organization.

FEDERAL INTERVENTION

Increased federal involvement in northern native communities after World War Two, intensifying in the 1960s, eventually divested missions of their involvement in health and

education. The goals of assimilation, at least in the forms initially conceived by missions, were not part of government initiatives. Service priorities shifted toward administrative inclusion of native people in the programs offered to the rest of Canadian society. In the provision of medical services, this involved a greater institutional presence in the North, while education programs made at least some effort to take into consideration the unique cultures and experiences of native peoples. The institutional presence of the federal government was also enhanced through reorganization of village politics by enforcing the establishment of elected Chiefs and Councils. A variety of formal administrations were active in the processes of village centralization and the development of new forms of native leadership.

By the beginning of the twentieth century, the James Bay Cree had largely recovered from the periodic waves of epidemics that accompanied early contact in the eighteenth and nineteenth centuries. But with a government drive toward sedentarization and administrative control of the northern native population, came many of the health problems associated with dense villages, poor housing, and an absence of sanitary infrastructure. Tuberculosis was rampant in many native communities, not just those of the subarctic. Young (1988: 40–41) reports that a survey of the Norway House Agency in northern Manitoba in the 1920s uncovered a tuberculosis mortality rate of 20/1,000, while the average mortality rate from all causes was approximately 25/1,000. An elderly woman I spoke with in Mistassini remembered the time following the centralization of the village in the 1940s, when makeshift government nursing stations set up in tents were used to treat those whose relatives could no longer care for them: "the old people...looked so bad, so lonely. You would see somebody, an old lady, lying there coughing and coughing.... When somebody got sick, you should have seen the flies. They crawled around their face, on their mouth, because they were so helpless."

The medical crises of village centralization were seen by some as an opportunity to display to the Indian the superiority of science and civilization. A 1912 report from a northern Indian agent already shows the link between native health services and the goal of assimilation: "A permanent medical officer at this point would be a great benefit to the Indians: nothing has a more civilizing effect upon them than a display of the white man's skill in healing, nothing convinces them more readily of the white man's interest in them" (cited in Young, 1988: 90).

In Fort George it was not until the late 1940s that this opportunity was acted upon. By 1950 a new thirty-two–bed hospital opened and was full to capacity from the outset, mainly with cases of tuberculosis. While the Catholic mission played a central part in the operation of this hospital, furnishing many of the nurses and, in 1964, one of the doctors, the federal government was increasingly active in all aspects of the provision of health care. In 1970, when another, larger hospital was constructed on Fort George, only two of the gray sisters remained to transfer their services to the now fully secularized institution.

One can speculate that federal government intervention in Cree villages, manifested in rapid centralization and the introduction of formal agencies, was also responsible for a change in the pattern of mental illness. Instead of the neuroses or psychotic episodes associated with winter isolation in the forest, the new villages would become settings in which emotional instability and despondency afflicted those previously unfamiliar with permanent sedentarization.

Whatever the cause of mental illness, one of the most dramatic changes in Cree medical history was the new method of intervention which made use of evacuation, often using police escort, to institutions in southern cities. As an elder in Mistassini remembered, "The RCMP [Royal Canadian Mounted Police] at that time used to fly into the community and take people away, strap them in leather ropes to hold the people down.... The medical profession at that time thought that the best place for these [emotionally disturbed] people was in institutions." Federal involvement in native medical services involved, for the first time in Cree territory, the use of force and incarceration as a strategy in healing.

Many of the changes brought about by government administration of health care were less dramatic than the system of psychiatric intervention would lead us to believe.

Church services, the most reliable venue in which many members of the community regularly gathered, sometimes included talks by the minister with messages from medical personnel on the availability of medical services and the importance of using them. Although the Cree had long been accustomed to a dual usage of indigenous healing with any available biomedical services, there was an effort by medical personnel in the communities to discourage those practices that were at odds with their views of appropriate care. The practice of bleeding by venesection (opening a vein) at the wrist or ankle, for example, eventually disappeared from the Cree system of healing because of biomedical hazards associated with the loss of blood during illness. Even today, however, nurses in Mistassini find that elders having blood samples taken at the clinic will sometimes make (unrequited) requests to have extra vials drawn, with the explanation that this would make them feel better.

Cree midwifery, though not actively targeted for eradication, involved risks and a loss of biomedical control that were most effectively overcome by encouraging clinic or hospital births. Midwives were women who had informally developed an expertise in assisting in childbirth, sometimes using natural remedies to control complications. Although lacking in specialized tools of diagnosis and intervention, Cree midwives possessed practical experience and personal knowledge of women and their families. And, as one narrative told over the Chisasibi radio shows, their approach to infant care was not inconsistent with the practices recommended by most public health practitioners: "The most important advice I got from [midwives at] the time I had my first child was that I must breast-feed her. This gives the child a better start in life. I had twelve children and I breast-fed them all."[4]

The logistical and social demands of childbirth in the formal system when hospitals became available were quite different. For those in isolated villages like Eastmain or Wemindji, childbirth in the formal medical system regularly

---

4. Excerpt from a radio narrative recorded in Chisasibi.

involved air travel to Fort George, Moosonee, or Chibouga-mou (a mining town near Mistassini, Québec). The trip, usu-ally undertaken around two weeks from their expected delivery, was an ordeal for heavily pregnant women who had, in some cases, never before flown in an airplane. Cree women began to make use of hospital facilities for childbirth in the 1960s. By 1977, the eve of implementation of the new James Bay Agreement, hospital admissions in the Cree re-gion included a rate of 571 hospitalizations relating to preg-nancy, childbirth, and follow-up to childbirth per 10,000 admissions, compared to 153 per 10,000 at the Montreal Gen-eral Hospital (Bernèche and Robitaille 1980: 23), a finding that reflects both the high birth rate among the Cree and their shift toward frequent use of hospital facilities for ob-stetrical procedures (see Magonet, n.d., 53–54 and Salisbury, 1986: 42).

Federal involvement in the health services of the Cree communities involved increasing the formalization of health administration and the ties to institutions in the South. Here one can see a departure from missionary activity. The com-plexity of the federal health system far exceeded the modest Church support given to the isolated and largely indepen-dent missionaries; and under formalized health care, chang-es to Cree culture were not encouraged through moral imperatives and sanctions as much as instrumental/techno-logical promises and legal sanctions. Cree health care be-came assimilated into a formal juridical system controlled by officials, legal experts, and medical professionals.

In the late 1960s and early 1970s the federal government also became much more involved in the formal education of native students. In 1971 the House Standing Committee on Indian Affairs accepted as a policy guideline the National Indian Brotherhood's statement, 'Indian Control of Indian Education.' Similar approval came from the Department of Indian and Northern Affairs in 1973. The two main purpos-es of this new policy orientation were to develop greater rec-ognition of aboriginal cultures in provincial and federal schools through the inclusion of native cultural content in curriculum materials and to include the use of native lan-guages and native teachers in schools where mostly native students were educated (Preston, 1979: 92). Under this new policy, the mission-operated boarding school in Fort George passed into federal control with lay teachers and administrative staff. But the new policy orientation was perhaps most tangibly realized in the Cree community of Waskaganish, where a grass-roots program of curriculum development called the 'Cree Way Project' was implemented from 1974 to 1976. John Murdoch, a school principal in Wemindji and later Waskaganish, had informally implemented the project several years before it received recognition and funding from the federal government. His approach to Cree education was to begin by teaching Cree syllabics in the primary grades and developing a curriculum that reflected the history, beliefs, and experience of hunting and trapping of the local community. With the eventual production of hundreds of mimeographed items in Cree syllabics, the Cree Way Project developed the foundation for the curriculum development and policy orientation of the Cree School Board that was to take over federal responsibility for Cree education in the late 1970s. It did not succeed, however, in developing materials for higher grades, a step that would have required extensive research into the semantic structure of the Cree language (Preston, 1979).

For high school education, Cree students had to go to urban centers in the south. More students went outside of Cree territory for their education, especially to Sault Sainte Marie in Ontario, with its schools' English-language curriculums. The expansion of educational services by the federal government was to have important implications for the major political developments of the 1970s. At the time when the Québec government was about to propose a major hydroelectric project in Cree territory, there was a small number of Cree high school graduates who had been through the experience of struggling for their education, leaving their homes to live in an alien, sometimes racist environment and against all odds achieve what they had set out to accomplish. As Salisbury points out, "When the challenge arose of doing something in reply to the threat of the James Bay project, these high school graduates felt that they should fight, even though most Cree initially were somewhat fatalistic" (1986: 126). A small circle of educated men, known to each other from their days in school together, with organizational skills, contacts with officials in government and university researchers, was "crucially placed, and highly motivated to organize what became a political movement" (Salisbury, 1986: 127). Although residential education included roughly equal enrollments of both sexes, very few young women went on to complete their educations outside their home villages. One woman, Violet Pachanos, who was among this circle of Crees educated in schools and colleges of the South, later became the first female chief in the James Bay region, serving two terms in Chisasibi in the early 1990s, and in September, 1996 became the first woman elected to a position of regional leadership, as Deputy Grand Chief of the Grand Council of the Crees.

Another of the more portentous forms of federal intervention in the affairs of native people did not have a precedent in missionary programs: the creation of the formal political institutions of Chief and Council. According to one Cree point of view, the institution of the chief is an extension of earlier leadership roles instituted mainly for the convenience of a bureaucratic white society otherwise unable to deal with semi-nomadic hunting families. Tallymen, or *'uuchimaau'*, the hunting leaders who were formally affiliated with trading posts, were in this sense prototypes of the later chiefs. The association between early chiefs and hunting leaders is so strong that the two roles are sometimes conflated. As Smally Petawabano, former chief of Mistassini, informed me, "The chief started actually when the first white men came in. We didn't call them chiefs, we just called them leaders. You could be *uuchimaau* because you're a real crack hunter." The authority of tallymen, however, in contrast to the broad role to be defined for village chiefs, was limited to management of each season's hunting and trapping activities. "The tallymen were always men of respect," Smally Petawabano remembers, "because they were the ones who managed the trapline harvest as well as the leaders in determining the hunting pattern that would happen that year."

In the 1930s a revised Indian Act was implemented in Canada's remote northern regions. This brought about a new resolve on the part of federal authorities to enforce earlier provisions in the Act that called for the creation of band councils in some of the isolated regions of the north. This resolve led to the creation for the James Bay Cree communities of the new positions of Chiefs and Councilors. In Cree settlements in which the egalitarian values of a dispersed hunting society were still emphasized and leadership based upon the respect given those with superior skill in the forest economy, the announcement that chiefs had to be elected was met with confusion and mild resistance. As Henry Mianscum, former chief of Mistassini, recalls, those living in the settlement in the 1930s, "didn't understand about the Indian Act...and they thought the Indian Act should not tell us how to appoint our chief." The first point of disagreement over the election rules set out in the Indian Act was a restriction of suffrage to those over twenty-one years of age. In times of famine among subarctic hunters it was sometimes the very young, the ten- to thirteen-year-old hunters, who would catch something that brought the camp back to health. Most sixteen year-old Cree were fully autonomous in their activities on the land. As one elder protested in his recollection of this time, "Saying that there is an age limit [to voting privileges] is not the Cree way." A minimum voting age of twenty-one was inconsistent with the level of responsibility expected from those who were much younger.

Although nothing could be done to alter the age restriction on the vote, some creativity took place in the form of the ballot. Rejecting as inappropriate for a largely non-literate society the idea of a standard paper ballot on which names of candidates were written, the people of Mistassini, in one early election, decided on a more personal format. As Smally Petawabano reported, "They opened a can for each [candidate] with his name on it.... So everyone came in with a penny. ... Each candidate was sitting with his own little tin, and they made sure the [voters] didn't throw more than one. And in the end they counted and announced the chief." In an even greater departure from formal election procedure related to me by Smally Petawabano, candidates for chief and council once used the classic lottery system of drawing straws to determine an election outcome, with the long 'stick' determining the chief, while other candidates became councilors, one councilor for every one hundred community members.

In the first decades of the chiefship, the Department of Indian Affairs paid infrequent visits to the villages, and the chief's official obligations were limited. Henry Mianscum explained that the functions of the chief were more social than 'political' in a formal sense: "In those days nobody knew what the role of the chief and council was. They just rubber stamped.... People came in with their own sets of letters and resolutions...And the chief just signed the papers." This absence of policy-development and decision-making responsibilities allowed the chief and councilors to devote their attention to the personal affairs and difficulties of their village constituency. Again Mianscum recalled:

> The chief became identified as the leader of the community. He was called upon to participate in all bereavements and he was the guest of honor for... weddings. He was involved in any social [problem] that was occurring. He was always there. He was the comforter. He was your friend.... There was nothing fancy about his mandate other than being a human being with a big heart.

The advice-giving role of the chief and councilors was called upon only when other avenues in the family had not resulted in resolution of an interpersonal problem. In such cases, Mianscum reported, "The first thing you know, the father of that family would say, 'Well let's go and talk to the chief.'"

One example of the arbitration activities of the early chief occurred in Mistissini in the 1940s when a young woman resisted an arranged marriage:

> There was an old man who wanted to marry a young teenage girl. The man was about sixty-five or sixty-six and the teenage girl was only about eighteen or nineteen years old.... At that time [some people in the community] said, "That's a bit too old for this man to marry this girl." Everybody talked

about it. Everybody put their mind to it.... Then the chief was the one who gave a direction, to make sure this didn't happen, and then everybody got together and they all agreed. In other words, no forced marriages for anyone.

This shows a consensus-building approach to the resolution of a controversy with broad implications. Rather than resort to the formal laws of non-native society or even tell people in a direct way what they should do, the chief provided a direction, articulating an opinion that eventually received wide approbation and became the basis for an informal social rule in the community.

The formalization of political office through enforcement of provisions in the Indian Act created a new realm of village leadership in Cree society built upon roles of those who managed activities in the forest. The tallymen maintained control over activities in the traplines, but a new role was created for organization and mediation in the villages. The chief and councilors were also *uuchimaau*, but their responsibilities were directed more toward the settled community than the forest. For some communities, federal regulation was accompanied by new infrastructures—schools, clinics, government housing, and government offices—and greater centralization of settlements which brought together families from widely scattered territories. The principal challenge of the new leadership was to bring people together in these new circumstances, to create new alliances and networks that would extend the principles of cooperation and reciprocity through rapidly growing villages. For the first decades of formal leadership, the tasks of chiefs and councilors were extensions of the social skills used in coordinating the activities of families in the forest. Challenging as it was, this situation was not to last long. In the 1970s a much more dramatic change in the qualifications and activities of Cree leaders took place in response to a provincial government with unprecedented ambitions to conquer the northern wilderness.

4

Negotiated Transformations

Québec is a vast hydroelectric plant in-the-bud, and every day millions of potential kilowatt-hours flow downhill and out to sea. What a waste!

Robert Bourassa, *Power from the North.*

And because [the river] rises a little outside the city, the Amaurotians have enclosed the head spring of it with strong fences and bulwarks.... From thence the water is diverted in all directions and brought down in canals of brick divers ways into the lower parts of the city.

Thomas More, *Utopia.*

Until the hydroelectric potential of northern Québec was realized and acted upon in the 1970s, the Cree of the Eastern James Bay had been isolated from many of the influences of resource extraction and the industrial economy. The climate has been a source of discomfort to those unaccustomed to the north ever since the first explorers ventured into the region. The winters are cold, with temperatures commonly plunging into the –40° Fahrenheit range as arctic air funnels south on the Hudson and James Bays. In the brief summer, the region is famous for its insect life, with black flies breeding prodigiously quantities in the running water and mosquitoes in the stagnant; either way, the unprepared become prey to hardy, voracious biting insects. The Cree, accustomed to this environment, had only to deal for the most part with fur traders, missionaries, a few rival trappers, but at no point did they face an invasion of settlers such as occurred, for example, with the westward expansion of the United States in the nineteenth century.

If a precise date has to be established for this relative stability to be permanently altered, it would probably be April 30, 1971 when the premier of Québec, Robert Bourassa, announced his plan for the 'Project of the Century', a $6 billion hydroelectric project to be built in the James Bay region, intended to create 125,000 jobs. The James Bay project was to involve the construction of dozens of dams on rivers in northern Québec which together would eventually produce 28,000 megawatts of electricity, enough to power New York City, making it the largest hydroelectric complex in North America. Much of the power was to be exported to the New England states through thousands of miles of power lines strung along rows of transmission towers. The scale of the project was heroic, and this in itself was one of its anticipated benefits. "It had been expected that the James Bay hydroelectric concept would inspire the citizens of Québec," Bourassa would later reflect (1985: 17–18). This was to be a unifying effort for the people of Québec, not just through anticipated economic prosperity, but more importantly the sustained common purpose necessary for creating monuments of human ingenuity.

The days following Bourassa's announcement of the James Bay project became a time of political awakening for several Cree leaders. Philip Awashish, a university student, first read about Premier Bourassa's plans for the development of the lands they occupied in a day-old copy of the Montreal *Star* in the mining town of Chibougamou (MacGregor, 1990: 60). Bringing this news to the attention of his former school mate, Billy Diamond, a young leader from Waskaganish, they suggested a gathering of chiefs in Mistissini to discuss a Cree response to the Hydro-Québec Project. This was the beginning of a series of political struggles that was to bring a group of young, formally educated Cree leaders to the forefront of Canadian and international efforts to secure the rights of indigenous peoples.

Hydro-electricity and the Goals of Extractive Industry

Contrasting approaches to the land and its resources is a basic theme that has recurred throughout the five centuries of relations between indigenous peoples and explorers, settlers, traders, miners, and loggers in the New World. William Cronon's study of the cultural patterns of land use in colonial New England describes some of the ways that asymmetries in the use of land between nomadic or semi-nomadic Indians and colonists aiming to reproduce the sedentary patterns of English farms and townships, led to dramatic ecological changes and a decline in the viability of the Indians' migratory subsistence strategies. The usurpation and 'improvement' of Indian lands was justified on the grounds that nomadic hunting and gathering did not constitute true 'ownership' of the land. "To European eyes," Cronon writes, "Indians appeared to squander the resources that were available to them. Indian poverty was the result of Indian waste: underused land, underused natural abundance, underused human labor" (1983: 56).

Political philosophy in the seventeenth century also reflected the virtues of cultivation and 'improvement'. In Locke's *Two Treatises of Government* it is made plain that ownership of land rightfully belongs to those who make proper use of it, that is to say, those who are able to extract resources from it most productively. The lands of America provide Locke with his most telling example: "I ask whether in the wild woods and uncultivated wast [sic] of America left to Nature, without any improvement, tillage or husbandry, a thousand acres will yield the needy and wretched inhabitants as many conveniencies of life as ten acres of equally fertile land doe [sic] in Devonshire where they are well cultivated?" (1988: 294). The original inhabitants of America, according to Locke, are impoverished in the midst of potential abundance for want of improvement by labor; and such improvidence makes it not only permissible but necessary for those capable of improving the land to take possession of it. The Pilgrim apologist Robert Cushman was to give this idea more poignant imagery when he described the land rotting and spoiled, "marred for want of manuring, gathering, ordering, etc." while the Indian occupants "do but run over the grass, as do also the foxes and wild beasts" (cited in Cronon, 1988: 56).

Bourassa's reasoning behind his commitment to mega-projects in the North fits almost seamlessly into early justifications for American settlement by Europeans. In his book, *Power from the North,* he writes, "What once appeared to be a forbidding and barren land, only sparsely populated by the Inuit and Cree, has become Québec's new frontier" (Bourassa, 1985: 2). The land, for Bourassa, is only sparsely populated, not improved by human labor, while the potentially energy-rich waters of powerful rivers flow unobstructed and unused into the sea. Nature itself, for Bourassa, possesses the same features—wildness, remoteness, uncontrolled savagery—that most of us are familiar with from stories of the American frontier: "It has long been my belief that Québec's economic strength lies in the development of its natural resources [and]...that to develop these resources would require conquering and taming the North" (Bourassa, 1985: 13). His vision of a prosperous Québec is dominated by the *idée fixe* of using technological sophistication and engineering marvels to alter and improve the wilderness, bringing resource extraction on a grand scale into a remote and, as he sees it, unused landscape.

There is also a strong element of cultural pride at work in the commitment to mega-projects in northern Québec. Hydroelectric construction in Québec is, as James Maxwell and his co-authors point out, "similar to the large-scale science or engineering projects undertaken in the past in the United States which contributed to regional and national pride because they involved cutting-edge engineering techniques and highly regarded leaders" (Maxwell et. al., 1996: 22). Bourassa similarly expresses pleasure at Québec's engineering accomplishments, especially the fact that New Yorkers routinely enjoy the benefits of Québec's power as they ride the subway or turn on the lights, oblivious to the dams producing energy far to the north (1985: 2). He adds another dimension to the satisfaction of meeting engineering challenges by taking nationalistic pride in both the culture and resources of Québec and its citizens' political will to make the project a reality:

> If Québec is unique in North America in its cultural character, it is also unique in its geography, climate, and, perhaps most important of all, its generous endowment of natural resources.... The primary obstacle to the projects proposed in this book will be political, but I have an unbounded confidence in the common sense and realism of my fellow Québecers. I share with them a profound attachment to Québec and a deep pride in its distinctive heritage and culture (Bourassa, 1985: 174).

For Bourassa, there is a close connection between northern mega-projects, pride in Québec's energy-rich natural environment, and Québecers' will to overcome natural and political obstacles to realize their ambition and genius.

But of course the overriding motivation behind mega-project construction is economic. Bourassa outlines the expected benefits of the Power from the North (Great Whale) project in terms of job creation, which would be roughly

The La Grande River, downstream from the La Grange 2 project (L-G 2) hydro-electric installation.

195,000 man-years of work in Québec over a ten-year period (1985: 130). During construction on the La Grande complex, Hydro-Québec paid a total of $5.6 billion in wages and used $4.6 billion (both figures in Canadian currency) worth of Québec goods and services. In return, Hydro-Québec's $8 billion in sales from the James Bay project to date has accounted for 5.6 percent of the province's Gross National Product (Maxwell et al., 1996: 20). Although Bourassa was never a secessionist, his support of home grown megaprojects shows that this is precisely the kind of economic initiative he believed necessary for Québec to realize its strength as an autonomous cultural and political entity.

THE JAMES BAY AGREEMENT

On May 5, 1972, the Cree and Inuit filed a joint representation to the Québec Superior Court to have the law creating the James Bay Development Society declared unconstitutional. Later that year, on October 27, the Cree and Inuit petitioned the court for a more immediate decision: a temporary injunction on construction at La Grande 2 and other sites pending a decision on the original legal action. On December 5, 1972 Judge Albert Malouf began presiding over the hearing concerning the temporary injunction. What should have been under normal circumstances a relatively simple process of deciding on an injunction became, as the press called it, 'The James Bay Trial', involving testimony from 167 witnesses over a six-month period (Richardson, 1991; Bourassa, 1985: 33). These witnesses included an assembly of experts—engineers, biologists, hydrologists, sociologists, anthropologists—but also less expected appearances by an altogether different form of expert: Cree and Inuit hunters, some of whom had traplines on land soon to be flooded. They probably imagined they would be asked to talk about the kind of life they led on the land, their relationship with animals, the importance these attachments had for them and their families, and the fears they had about losing their way of life to bulldozers and rising waters. The actual court procedure, as described by Boyce Richardson, probably did not correspond with any form of discourse the Cree and Inuit witnesses had ever previously encountered. James O'Reilly, a lawyer for the Cree and Inuit plaintiffs, complained, "The cross-examiners were wanting the Indian witnesses to be like computers, to produce all sorts of figures and documents that should more properly be sought elsewhere, and...were...trying to confuse the Native witnesses" (Richardson, 1991: 41). But not all of the witnesses became confused by this procedure. For example, when asked if he kept track of the fish he caught, George Pachano, a hunter from Fort George, replied crisply, "It was not intended by the Creator who created the fish that the Indian should keep track of all the fish that he kills" (in Richardson, 1991: 41).

On November 15,1973, almost a year after the start of the hearing, Judge Malouf handed down his decision, a 360-page judgment, granting the Cree and Inuit the temporary injunction they sought. Work on the dam sites in the North ground to a halt. The same day, however, the James Bay Development Corporation, the James Bay Energy Corporation, and Hydro-Québec filed an appeal, requesting a suspension of the injunction until the Malouf decision could be formally appealed. A week later, when the Québec Court of Appeals agreed to this temporary suspension, work on the construction sites resumed.

Despite a favorable decision from Judge Malouf, the Cree and Inuit legal initiative to stop the James Bay project became mired; and in the meanwhile construction was continuing. Under these circumstances, they had little choice but to negotiate. The Québec government was well prepared. By November 25, 1973, John Ciaccia, a special representative to Premier Bourassa, had already prepared an eleven-point offer to the Cree and Inuit which included some modifications to the project, some environmental protection measures, guarantees of hunting, fishing and trapping rights, and monetary compensation of $100 million (Bourassa, 1985: 34). This began a complex process of negotiation between three main political bodies: the Québec government and its provincially-owned development corporations, the federal government, and representatives of the Cree and Inuit. Early in the negotiation process, the

Crees were represented by the Indians of Québec Association, at the time the most influential Native political organization in Québec, but in September, 1974 the Crees formed their own political body, the Grand Council of the Crees (of Québec). The Inuit were represented by the Northern Québec Inuit Association.

Cree negotiators had as their highest priority protection of the land and the viability of the forest way of life, reflecting the view of one elder that this is the real source of wealth and security: "[The] white man wants to put money in the bank and once he gets his money in the bank he feels secure, his children are secure because he has got something to look forward to. And its the same thing for us [with] the land. Its just like putting money in the bank. There will always be something for us, for our young generation. And we feel secure also." Kenny Blacksmith, Deputy Grand Chief of the Grand Council of the Crees, in a statement to the Joint Energy Committee at the Massachusetts State House in March, 23, 1995, expressed the view that protection of the land continues to be a political goal with the highest priority, and that the James Bay Agreement did not meet his expectations: "We received pennies an acre for the land that was destroyed and taken from us, and this does not account for the economic, social and other damage. But we would give up this once-only compensation without a moment's thought if we could protect and maintain our lands, our sustainable economy, and our way of life" (1995: 2).

Achieving such protections in the context of guarantees of social and economic autonomy, rather than an uncompromising opposition to the project, seems to have been the general orientation of the early Cree response to the James Bay project. This was, Harvey Feit (1985) argues, arrived at by regional leaders in consultation with elders rather than the outcome of Cree dependency on consultants and lawyers. The process of negotiation began, according to Feit, with an effort to achieve some form of consensus through community feedback, especially by attempts on the part of the first regional leaders to receive guidance from chiefs and other elders concerning the general, long-term goals of political action. The advice they received was "to achieve long-term reconciliation rather than ever-increasing confrontation" (Feit, 1985: 59).

The outcome of the negotiations that began, from the Cree point of view, with the premises of protection, autonomy, and reconciliation is the James Bay and Northern Québec Agreement, signed in 1975. It provides a cash settlement which now amounts to approximately $255 million. Some of the services previously provided by the federal government were reorganized in the Agreement to provide a measure of administrative autonomy for the Cree within Québec's government and legal jurisdictions. This includes the Cree School Board, run by elected representatives of the Cree communities, and the Cree Board of Health and Social Services of James Bay. It also established local law enforcement agencies, and changed Band Councils into 'local governments' based upon a municipal model. The most important concern of Cree leaders, protection of the land and hunting way of life, was addressed (although not entirely to the Cree leadership's satisfaction, as we will see below) by the provision of land grants in each of the original eight communities,[1] totaling approximately 2,158 square miles (of a territory consisting of some 215,000 square miles[2]). This land (referred to as Category 1) is defined in the Agreement as being "for the exclusive use and benefit of the...James Bay Cree bands" (Government of Québec, 1976: 55) and falls into the jurisdiction of Band Councils consisting of elected chiefs and councilors. Each village with its Band Council and surrounding land grants officially constitutes a 'municipality' under the terms of the Québec Cities and Towns Act (Salisbury, 1986: 65). The Agreement also provides the Cree with specific rights over the adjacent territories, totaling some 25,130 square miles. These lands are intended to provide Cree hunters with exclusive hunting and fishing rights, but, according to the terms of the Agreement, may be appro-

---

1. Ouje-Bougoumou, established in 1990, has not been provided a land grant.
2. This is based on the definition of the James Bay territory under the terms of the Development Act (James Bay Energy Corporation 1988: 4).

priated by Québec for development purposes, subject to a replacement of the appropriated lands or some other form of mutually agreed–upon compensation. Even with these territories under Cree control, the greatest proportion of what is claimed as Cree territory, roughly 188,000 square miles, fell into Québec control, giving mining and logging enterprises a framework around which to orient their activities, and giving hunters from the South rights to use lands that, with the construction of roads, they could now access more freely.

The Agreement establishes a regional governing body, the Cree Regional Authority (CRA), which controls investment of compensation funds and, with the consent of villages, coordinates and administers development programs that apply to the region as a whole. The Executive Committee of the CRA is composed of all band chiefs and one representative from each band council, a system that closely integrates regional and village politics. The range of programs handled by the CRA is extremely broad and, as Salisbury's description shows, the CRA office in Val d'Or is often a hive of activity:

> In one room is that latest shipment of tamarack duck decoys, awaiting distribution to Montreal; in another room a group of village representatives are discussing the progress of their rehousing plan; the main CRA office is busy planning next year's program for economic development, relocation of the affiliated organizations to particular villages, and all the routine administration of current programs; expected in on tomorrow morning's plane from Montreal are the CRA lawyers to discuss legal negotiations with Québec and Ottawa regarding health schemes…and today the secretariat is busy preparing documentation. The switchboard is constantly being asked if Sam or Jimmy or Fred is in town yet, coming to a meeting from one of the villages, and to pass on a message when he comes in (1986: 66).

The CRA has administrative jurisdiction over a wide range of regional affairs, including shared responsibility with Band Councils of investment of the $255 million settlement. The CRA does not, however, handle many of the political activities that affect the region as a whole. The Grand Council of the Crees has responsibility for regional politics. It is a parallel governing body to the CRA, and is composed of essentially the same Executive Committee of village chiefs and council representatives. The Grand Council differs structurally from the CRA, however, in being led by a regionally elected Grand Chief who is authorized to speak on behalf of all Cree people. The CRA is the administrative wing of Cree government, responsible for implementing programs, while the Grand Council is the political wing, a forum for discussion of policies with regional implications, equipped with the expertise to negotiate with outside agencies and coordinate resistance to programs and development strategies seen to threaten Cree interests.

The Agreement also established the Income Security Program (ISP), which provides a government subsidy for those who pursue the hunting way of life. In the early 1990s, a little more than 30 percent of the James Bay Crees were enrolled in this program. To be eligible for a guaranteed annual income, which averaged $11,237 per household in 1991, the participants are required to spend a minimum of 120 days in the bush, and cannot combine regular wage employment with ISP benefits. Hunters on the ISP can, however, supplement their incomes with seasonal wage labor as long as they follow the general, and somewhat vague, rule that "the practice of harvesting constitutes a way of life for the beneficiaries" (Cree Hunters and Trappers Income Security Board, 1991: 15). Since eligibility in the ISP is determined by the activities of the self-declared head of the household, their dependents do not have to reside the minimum number of days in the bush, allowing children to attend school while living with relatives or one of their parents in the community.

As with any program involving cash disbursements from government, it is possible to find abuses of the Income Security Program. Cree people in the communities can point to some receiving their ISP cheques who do not come even close to spending the minimum number of days in the bush camps. Others have remarked upon the fact that many cabins are constructed near highways and that, even with the advantages of snowmobiles and all-terrain vehicles, some hunters do not venture out into remote regions. Despite such criticism, however, Cree hunters continue to be productive. The Cree Trapper's Association's big game survey in its 1994 Annual Report (1994: 12) shows that 566 caribou and 315 moose were taken by Cree hunters in 1993–1994, while in the same year a total harvest of 3,686 beaver, 445 mink, 330 otter and 985 muskrats were among the prominent indicators of viable trapping activity (1994: 10).

One of the main obstacles to Cree hunting under the new regime is seen as the intrusion of non-Native sports hunters, which in the Waswanipi area for example, is endangering the moose population by over-hunting. According to the Grand Council of the Crees, this is occurring because obligations of the Québec Environment Ministry under the James Bay Agreement are not being met. Bill Namagoose, executive director of the Grand Council, expressed the view that the Québec government did not enforce its restrictions on the moose hunt because of a reluctance to anger separatist voters in the community of sportsmen before the referendum on Québec separation that took place on October 30, 1995 (*The Nation*, 1995c: 7).

The signing of the James Bay Agreement was the prelude to a complete reorganization of administration and government in the Cree territory of Québec. The Agreement fulfilled two major purposes for the Québec government: it cleared the way for extractive development of the North, mainly in the form of massive hydro-electric projects, and it clarified jurisdiction over the native people of its territory for whom federal responsibility was ambiguous and provincial jurisdiction ill-defined. John Ciaccia, special provincial representative in the James Bay negotiation, points to the importance of native assimilation into the provincial system in his statement of the philosophy of the Agreement: "Until now, Québec's presence in the North has not been complete. Today we are completing and reaffirming this presence. The Government of Québec has taken the opportunity presented by these negotiations to reorganize the territory, and to set up the institutions and structures that will give substance to the role that it intends to fulfill" (Ciaccia,

1991: xv). The precise nature of this role is left unstated. In terms of administrative change, however, the substance of Ciaccia's vision has been fulfilled. Schools and hospitals under federal jurisdiction in native communities were transferred to the jurisdiction of Québec. Regional native organizations established in the Agreement, jointly financed by federal and provincial governments, were soon to operate under the control of Québec's policies and procedures.

Hydro-Québec has also portrayed in glowing terms the James Bay Agreement and the development projects associated with it. A document entitled 'James Bay: Development, Environment and the Native Peoples of Québec', produced by Hydro-Québec for publicity purposes, points to improvements in health care and social services, the creation of a Cree School Board run by the elected representatives of the Cree communities, the founding of the Cree Hunters and Trappers Income Security Program (ISP) which provides subsidies to beneficiaries who follow the hunting lifestyle, a network of 950 miles of highways and secondary roads which provide hunters with access to remote territories, the construction of modern homes and municipal infrastructures, and the promise of profit from tourists who will be attracted to a now-accessible region with bountiful hunting and fishing resources (Hydro-Québec, 1989: 7–11).

The Crees have taken a view of the Agreement that stands in stark contrast to the optimism of the Québec government and Hydro-Québec spokespeople. With construction on the La Grande project ongoing during the period of negotiation, Cree leaders felt they had little choice but to participate and compromise. Chief Billy Diamond, one of the principal Cree negotiators of the Agreement, has pointed out that with the imminent threat of destruction of rivers and flooding of vast areas of Cree hunting territories, there was little choice but to negotiate with federal and provincial authorities to gain what concessions were available before the opportunity was lost. One of the conditions imposed on the Cree in the negotiation process, however, was unilateral extinguishment of Cree rights, most importantly, rights over the exclusive use of land. "Not only did the negotiators come in with [surrender and extinguishment] as a condition which was not subject to discussion or debate," Diamond commented, "but Canada made it clear that if we did not proceed with the agreement process, unilateral legislation would have been imposed on us in any case" (cited in Grand Council of the Crees, 1995: 253).

Sovereign Injustice, a document produced by the Grand Council of the Crees based on a submission to the United Nations Commission on Human Rights in 1992, also expresses disappointment at government insistence that the Cree and Inuit negotiators of the Agreement relinquish fundamental rights, which include control over use of the major part of Cree territory that is excluded from land grants, for essential services. Provision of schools, health services, law enforcement, public utilities and sanitation services were tied to the relinquishment of rights pertaining to lands in order to make the northern region of Québec available for development. "Since the James Bay Crees and Inuit had no choice but to improve their "Third World" conditions, Québec and Ottawa chose to insensitively exploit this most vulnerable position" (Grand Council of the Crees, 1995: 258). One of the terms of the Agreement that has been the focus of controversy and litigation also associates the James Bay and Northern Québec agreement with large-scale projects that are insensitive to aboriginal needs and social conditions. Section 8.1.3 cites the possibility of future projects and attempts to absolve the government signatories of responsibility for the social impacts this might have including, "It is recognized that there exists a possibility of future hydroelectric developments in the Territory.... It is agreed that these known projects...shall be considered as future projects subject to the environmental regime only in respect to ecological impacts and that sociological factors or impacts shall not be grounds for the Crees and/or Inuits to oppose or prevent the said developments" (Government of Québec, 1976: 111).

This term in the Agreement is considered a form of cultural genocide that violates both the Canadian Charter of Rights and Freedoms, the Universal Declaration of Human Rights, and the draft United Nations Declaration on the Rights of Indigenous Peoples, all of which, in one form or another, call for the right to life, liberty, and security of the person (Grand Council of the Crees, 1995: 268–269). Land grants and the ISP, according to this view, are insufficient to protect the Cree way of life in the face of further large-scale development.

Even the provision of essential services under the James Bay Agreement is sometimes seen by Cree political leaders and administrators to be inadequate and inequitable. A justice system that relies heavily on punishment, especially incarceration, rather than healing has been criticized as being out of touch with the social realities of remote aboriginal communities, prompting an independent study by the Grand Council of the Crees into the potential for an autonomous Cree justice system (McDonnell, 1992). One form of perceived punishment is derived from the power of the Youth Protection Act to remove children from their parents. Despite an understanding of the need to protect children, people in the Cree communities commonly express dismay at the power social workers have to remove children from their parents and place them in foster homes. According to Article 38 of the Youth Protection Act, social service intervention can take place when the security and development of a child are seen to be endangered, and the more precise conditions into which endangerment of security and development falls are extremely wide-ranging, including, "mental and affective development...threatened by lack of appropriate care," and parental behavior that "creates a risk of physical and moral danger to the child" (Government of Québec, 1984, Article 38). Among the many people I spoke with during social service research in Mistassini and Chisasibi, there seemed to be a great willingness to forgive and an even greater mistrust of the formal mechanisms of apprehension, judgment, and incarceration. Rather than resorting to punishment, many Cree people seem to be looking for healing and reconciliation, qualities they hope will be found in the ways elders once handled social and individual crises before the process of administrative formalization was accelerated by the James Bay Agreement (Niezen, 1993b: 234–235).

Besides what were widely perceived as ill-considered applications of non-native rules and policies to aboriginal institutions, some of the formal services provided for in the

Agreement were difficult to implement and continue to be under-funded. Albert Diamond, former treasurer of the Grand Council of the Crees, recalls the difficulties involved in getting federal and Québec governments to commit to implementing several key projects and programs, including the Cree School Board, the Cree Housing Corporation, and the Cree Health Board. "In many cases," Diamond reports, "it took months and months of educating and arguing, just trying to convince government officials that they had to develop a new program, that they had to go to their respective treasury boards and get the money" (1988: 116). In the establishment of the Cree School Board, for example, the Cree spent over $600,000 from their own funds between 1976 and 1978 because of the urgency in establishing the program. But subsequent requests to the government for reimbursement were refused. "Their position was that they would make the budgets available for operations only, and only when the personnel had been recruited" (Diamond, 1988: 116).

The transfer of health care to the autonomous Cree Board of Health and Social Services of James Bay was also hampered by government fiscal restraint, limiting the services that could be provided in the Cree communities. Chief Billy Diamond has sharply criticized the Québec government for its failure to honor some of the central service-oriented terms of the Agreement: "We worked in good faith with the government to provide a reasonable and effective plan to implement section 14 of the Northern Québec Agreement [dealing with health and social services].... To a great extent, this plan has not been implemented despite the promises of Québec to do so. The government is sabotaging their part of the agreement by withholding the resources to allow the board to adequately carry out its role" (cited in Lechky, 1991: 197). Besides the frustration of not seeing a promised program realized in the way it was initially envisaged, government inaction in the implementation of the Agreement added substantially to its cost for the Crees and the federal and Québec governments. Numerous meetings between Cree representatives and government officials in Ottawa, Montreal, Québec, Val D'Or, and the Cree communities required payment of travel expenses, operating costs of offices, and fees for lawyers and consultants. And as Albert Diamond notes sardonically: "All these costs had to be covered while we sat and argued about what a certain clause or a certain section meant" (1988: 116).

Complications in the implementation of the Agreement were to foreshadow the Crees' later lack of confidence in the potential of an autonomous Québec to assume treaty obligations of the federal government. Québec's ambitious plans for development, avoidance of environmental and social impact assessments, unilateral creation on Cree territory of a 'municipality' in the form of the Société de Développement de la Baie James—all these trends or indications of trends came to be seen as very real threats to the Cree way of life if an independent Québec were to acquire unlimited control of the North and its aboriginal inhabitants.

But a more immediate concern in the early 1980s was to overcome the administrative obstacles to resolving the self-destruction and violence that followed from road construction, loss of land to reservoirs, and community relocation. Cree administrators and political leaders were challenged to overcome the crises of a society in which the elastic limit of adjustment to change had been stretched to the breaking point.

5

Crisis and Accommodation

All major changes are like death.... You can't see to the other
side until you are there.

Michael Crichton, *Jurassic Park.*

For Robbie Louttit, a defining moment in his career as a
police officer in the new village of Chisasibi occurred early
one morning in January, 1983 as he was driving along the
perimeter road. A small movement in the drifting snow
caught his attention. Shifting the truck in reverse he moved
back for a second look and discovered that what might have
been mistaken for a chunk of snow was actually a six-
month-old infant dressed only in a disposable diaper.
Scooping the baby up and wrapping it inside his coat next
to his body, he could see that the door to a nearby house was
standing ajar. Inside, he found a young couple lying uncon-
scious on the living room floor, the residue of a drinking
party scattered around them.

At the same time that alcoholism, child neglect, and juvenile crime were among the most serious behavior problems in the community, efforts to intervene by the police
and social services were thwarted by suspicion and resent-
ment toward what were seen as 'outside' agencies of enforcement. When one non-native couple from the South

accepted jobs in the new health and school boards in the early 1980s, they were given housing in a troubled part of Chisasibi, where groups of up to a hundred teenagers at a time would 'walk the road', roaming up and down the perimeter road with no other aim than to drink and 'party' with friends. As a social worker with the health board, the husband's itinerary would be posted in the hospital, making it possible for anyone to see when he was out of town. On one such occasion, early in the morning while his wife and daughter were by themselves, a group of about thirty teenagers surrounded the house. The first rock they threw smashed through the window of the living room, scattering glass everywhere, leaving a dent in the ceiling tile. As the woman and her daughter retreated to the hallway for safety, every window in the house was systematically broken. In discussions of the incident that followed, it was understood as an intentional threat to the new social worker who had been hired to control a crisis situation with the youth.

Those who remember this time have different ideas about what caused such neglect, violence, and lack of control. A relatively common answer is that ready access to alcohol changed the lives of those who had once lived in more peaceful isolation. Thus, the 400 mile road constructed in the mid-1970s linking Fort George to Mattagami suddenly opened up the community to towns in the south, making it possible to spend a night in the South and return with a carload of alcohol.

For some, it was the trauma of relocation to Chisasibi which started the trouble. Because new fluctuations in the level of the La Grande River caused by hydro-electric installations were seen by experts to create a risk of erosion, the community of Fort George was asked to vote on whether or not to relocate to a new site on the mainland. Although this decision divided the community, the combination of environmental threat and government promise led to a vote in favor of relocation. In 1980, the new community of Chisasibi was officially established. The relocation and the period that followed were emotionally unsettling for many people, creating anxiety among those unused to such intentional proximity to neighbors, erasing the individuality of owner-constructed homes, and providing a more anonymous setting for binge drinking.

Others looked to the land for the answer and saw a decline in young peoples's participation in forest life, despite the ISP, as a source of restlessness and uncertainty about their future that made them turn to gas sniffing, drugs, alcohol, and the false security of 'walking the road'. Those attending high school in Chisasibi, who often stayed in foster homes while their own families remained in the villages, had little chance to learn forest skills through the long apprenticeship needed to be self-sufficient. At the same time an official (and probably underestimated) jobless rate of 14 percent for men and 11 percent for women,[1] concentrated among those between sixteen and twenty-five years old, added to the sense of pessimism among youth.

During the worst period of crisis, fledgling Cree administrations were given the responsibility of turning things around. Elders, who once were turned to for intervention in behavior problems and family disputes based on their knowledge of values and etiquette, were unfamiliar with such problems as addictions and suicide. These came into the purview of such organizations as the Chisasibi Police and the Cree Board of Health and Social Services of James Bay. Especially in the early years of regional autonomy, rules and procedures legislated in non-native society were applied unchanged to the isolated and culturally unique Cree communities of the North. Some alleviation of the social crisis occurred when helping agencies were seen to be less dominated by 'white-man's thinking', had acquired greater trust, and had built stronger links to such values of forest life as self-reliance, cooperation, and respect toward elders. An insistence on the inclusion of local tradition in formal agencies, and formal support of forest life itself, are important aspects of the Cree response to the social pathol-

---

1. Figures from the 1981 census. As with all government unemployment statistics, these figures do not represent those who have not entered the work force.

ogy that followed hydro-electric construction and village centralization.

THE SOCIAL AFTERMATH

Fort George Island, in the mouth of the La Grande River, shows the remains of what was once a dispersed but active community. The half-dozen families who refused to move when a dam was to be constructed twenty miles upstream still live here during summer and fall while the river is navigable. During other times of year all but a diehard few move to Chisasibi on the mainland because fluctuating water levels from the dam make ice unstable and the river too dangerous to cross. The places they call home are the few intact cabins that remain among the broken foundations of relocated houses and the abandoned shells of homes not worth moving but whose erstwhile residents have painted 'do not touch' on their outside walls in bold letters, messages left by the owners not so much for possible trespassers as they are left-over reminders to wrecking crews that these dwellings were to be left intact. Here the houses or their ruins, and the bulldozed and buried remains of the school, hospital, and Hudson's Bay store, are spaced widely apart along the shore of the river.

One of the most dramatic changes to occur in any Cree village in recent decades was the relocation in 1980 of the community from Fort George Island to the new village of Chisasibi on the mainland. Some of the older buildings in Chisasibi, including the Catholic church, were relocated from Fort George, but many buildings in Chisasibi are relatively new, including a hospital, commercial center, school, arena, administrative center, and recreation facility. Hunters once gathered in the summer months to socialize on the shore of the La Grande River on Fort George Island, sitting along hitching posts for freighter canoes, smoking, chatting, and playing checkers. Now they meet in the commercial center in an open lobby area surrounded by a cafeteria, two grocery stores, a post office, and a tourist agency, where the noise and activity during peak hours at noon and after

A young girl plays near the ruins of an abandoned home on Fort George Island.

school are enough to have earned its nickname, 'the stock market'.

There is a reluctance among many to talk about life in Chisasibi in the years following relocation. A rash of suicides among young people went largely unnoticed by the outside world, but those who remember this time remain deeply affected. Parties lasting from several days to a week became the social vehicles for binge drinking that wreaked havoc on the health of individuals and the stability of families. An officer for the Chisasibi tribal police recalls that "there were shifts when…about every minute there was a phone call." Break-ins, especially in the apartments housing workers from the school or hospital, were common. Even the police station, left empty for several hours while officers were preparing for the semi-annual goose hunt, was broken into for its cache of confiscated alcohol.

The connection between this kind of behavior and the transformations brought about by relocation and large-scale development are not at all well understood. What happens to the social world of people who rapidly exchange the hunting and fishing lifestyle for salaried labor or dependency on unemployment or welfare? Those who favor large-scale projects see the opportunities afforded by formal employment and new Cree administrations. Hydro-Québec, initially intending to train 300 Crees and hire 150, has trained only 80 and, in 1996 had 12 full-time Cree employees, 10 temporary workers, and 32 on recall if jobs become available (*The Nation,* 1996a: 7). Despite such employment figures, Robert Boyd, former president of Hydro-Québec and founder of the La Grande project of the 1970s, spoke glowingly of the social benefits of the project: "Today the Crees are more numerous, better educated and, finally, stronger. And we deserve some of the credit for this happy evolution" (*The Gazette,* 1992b).

Yet the reasons for the 'social pathology' following relocation stand as questions that remain to be answered. Perhaps one reason for the absence of non-partisan assessments of the social consequences of hydro-electric development is that social impacts, far more than environmental consequences, are difficult to substantiate. Arguments which point to indicators of social disequilibration such as suicide, alcoholism, and family violence as resulting from the impact of the La Grande complex are vulnerable because they cannot connect 'social pathology' with large-scale development. Lacking statistics to show behavior patterns before road construction and the James Bay Agreement, a counter-argument could easily be made that it is just as well if the Cree economy changes, that this would bring these people more into the modern world where they would become useful citizens instead of isolated hunters and trappers living out-of-step with contemporary life. Any suggestion that social problems result from development can be seen as being illusory—it is rather underdevelopment that causes social pathology. Jobs, according to this perspective, would be the best way to help the Indian, and the only way to provide jobs is to develop the North in all ways possible.

There are several ways that the social aftermath of relocation and mega-project construction can be documented. Perhaps the most straightforward is to begin with environmental changes and note their immediate impact on human life. In the case of the La Grande project, one of the most dramatic impacts on the Cree lifestyle was the discovery in 1982 that flooded organic material under reservoirs stimulates the formation of methyl mercury which, entering the food chain, is associated with birth defects and neurological disorders. Fish was a staple 'bush food' in the Cree diet. It was usually the first solid food given to infants and one of the most important subsistence resources throughout an individual's life in the forest, comprising roughly a quarter of the Cree diet. Surveys near the La Grande complex in the early 1980s showed that 64 percent of Cree residents had mercury levels classified as unsafe by standards of the World Health Organization (Maxwell et. al., 1996: 8). Hydro-Québec's assessment of the problem stresses the temporary nature of dangerous levels of contamination: "With time, this phenomenon diminishes and Hydro-Québec's existing reservoirs in the James Bay area should return to their natural state in ten to twenty years" (1989: 15). The length of time Hydro-Québec cites for contaminated waters to return to their 'normal state', however, is unsupported by evidence. Meanwhile, a finding of the Mercury Surveillance Program, established in 1986 between Hydro-Québec and the Cree Board of Health, points to a continuing problem, especially with consumption of large, predatory species of fish like pike and lake trout: "the exposure of the Eastmain Crees has increased excessively during the summer of 1992. It is believed that the increase is due to fishing expeditions to the inland lakes. These fishing expeditions have brought back species of fish which were more contaminated by mercury" (Cree Board of Health, 1993: 1). Dietary limits on fish were strongly advocated by the mercury program, but as the findings from Eastmain show, this advice is not always followed. Among the results of the discovery of methyl mercury in the food chain was a new phrase in the Cree language, *nimas aksiwin*, 'fish disease', along with a perception among the Crees living near affected reservoirs or rivers that an important bush food was now unsafe, or 'contaminated'. This perception has in itself altered patterns of subsistence, increasing a trend in the Cree diet toward consumption of store-bought foods much higher in sugar and saturated fat than 'bush food'.

Such dramatic changes to the land as flooding and contamination of fish can only lead to a sense of sorrow or spiritual malaise among those accustomed to a careful scrutiny of human relationships with animals and the environment. This is borne out by a more immediate form of evidence of social impact: the testimony of those directly affected by the rapid pace of change following hydro-electric development. One hunter who lost his trapline to the creation of the La Grande 2 reservoir, for example, had this to say about the experience:

> Since they flooded my land, my trapline, there's not a single day that I don't think about it. I feel so sad about it. [It was] one thing I couldn't understand; I don't think I'll ever understand. One reason why I feel so bad is knowing that my land is flooded forever, that I will never see it come back [to] what it was like before they flooded it. I am sure of that, and I am sure that I won't be able to show my grandchildren what my land was like when I was living off [it] hunting. That's the biggest change I ever saw in my life.[2]

The relocation of Fort George residents to the new village of Chisasibi was another of the traumatic episodes resulting from the La Grande project. One feeling about this event is described by a member of a relocated household: "Half of us [the older generation], our childhood memories are on the island, so that means when you have to move from a place where you have grown up, half of you is missing." Another person contrasts the social atmosphere of Fort George and Chisasibi:

> On the Island we used to visit each other more and we used to know where everybody lived and we

---

2. Interview in Chisasibi, 20 August, 1992 translated from Cree by Juliet Bearskin.

The Commercial Center in Chisasibi.

walked from one end of the community to the other because everything was scattered all over the place…. But here [in Chisasibi] you have everything centralized and here we don't visit anymore and we don't share kind words with each other. We pass each other as if we were in downtown Montreal.

Many Crees, not just social service professionals, observed that relocation was accompanied by an increased incidence of individual and family crises. There is a widespread perception in Chisasibi and other Cree communities that a generation has emerged that is out of touch with traditional values, a situation that has been created by a strong shift toward reliance on formal institutions and closer contact with southern culture. Violet Pachanos, former chief of Chisasibi, makes just such an observation: "I see the difference in the young people and the way we were brought up. Its a completely different lifestyle. I feel that the discipline is not there for the children. I feel they're not made to know or understand why they should contribute. Everything is there for them…. [T]he kids don't seem to know what to do with themselves." The problems of discipline and communication of values seem to be more easily handled in the forest environment. In the bush, there are, above all, practical limitations to inappropriate behavior. How can a young person commit a serious legal offense or nourish a drug or alcohol addiction while living in a bush camp? And how can children be neglected while living in close quarters with several families connected by relations of kinship or friendship? As James Bobbish, General Manager of the Cree Board of Health and Social Services, explains: "The bush tends to be a natural disciplinarian.... [Young people] know they can't hang out in sub-zero weather in the middle of winter. But when they come into the community, the same family, the same parents, do not have that sense of control and sense of comfort with the community."

Narrative testimony can cover an extremely wide range of topics. Elders in particular tend not to be pinned down by specific questions but let their remarks range over their entire life experience, often covering issues of concern only indirectly. In a broadcast I once heard on Chisasibi's community radio, for example, the problem of bears at the village landfill was seen by an elder as embodying many of the ills faced by the new community. The elder did not himself explain why he felt this way, although it was not difficult for most of his listeners to extrapolate his message: their meat is inedible, tainted by their landfill diet, representing a decline in the productivity of the land as civilization finds its way into the North; they are spiritually powerful animals wandering uncomfortably close to human habitation where any wild animal unwary of man is a particular source of concern. Not every listener, however, is so informed that the testimony they hear makes sense or the priorities of the narrators placed in its proper context. If the importance of the forest economy is to be properly understood, more evidence must be presented, data that go beyond testimony—that can be dismissed as irrelevant, partisan, or inaccurate.

An especially clear example can be found in the records of local administrations. By its very nature, the process of incorporating native communities in ambitious programs of development and resource extraction involves the bureaucratization of previously informal activity, a process that sometimes leaves evidence of the ways in which changes to the natural world and community environments are affecting a society as a whole.

The frequency of social problems in the Cree communities is especially clearly reflected in social service records. These were the subject of a study conducted by Niezen and St. Jean (1988) in the eight (before the addition of Oujebougamou in 1990) communities of the James Bay Cree in an effort to better understand social service problems and procedures. The most common diagnostics in these files include: young offenders (minors who have committed criminal offenses), behavior problems at school, behavior problems at home, drug abuse, alcohol abuse, attempted suicide, neglect of children, family and/or marital problems, and adoption. During the administrative period from April 1, 1986 to March 31, 1987, there were between 687 and 759 active social service files for a population of 8,605 individuals. It is safe to say that such a high incidence of individual and family crisis handled by social service professionals supports more informal observations that the communities have experienced profound social problems in the years following the implementation of the La Grande project and the James Bay Agreement.

More alarming than the mere frequency of individual and family disturbances is the fact that formal social service intervention is overwhelmingly concerned with youth. Young people, aged eighteen and younger, experience the widest range of problems and take up most of the energy of social service workers of any age group. Those between the ages ten and nineteen made up 25.8 percent of the total population (8,605) of the Cree communities in 1986, yet for the same period this group was represented in 44.5 percent of social service files. This kind of evidence supplements narrative testimony by providing a rough measure of social crisis. In this case, social service records amply confirm local observations that in the decade following the implementation of the James Bay mega-project and the relocation or centralization of villages, a generation emerged that seems to have lost a close connection with the forest lifestyle and is deeply affected by the lack of self-esteem and identity that this can bring about.[3]

Finally, an indirect way to understand social crisis is to consider the effectiveness of strategies that are being used to alleviate it. If the community has developed successful ways of handling the disruption that follows from such things as village relocation, the loss of hunting territory, or the even greater trauma following a suicide, it can prevent a downward spiral of unresolved grief, substance abuse, family violence, and 'suicide clusters.' Workers in agencies of healing or enforcement often have important things to say about what causes social patterns of violence and self-destruction and whether or not their programs are effective in making desired changes.

One of the obstacles to healing that was especially overwhelming in the years immediately following the implementation of regional autonomy was the relatively straightforward issue of administrative efficiency. Wertman (1983), in an assessment of the James Bay Agreement, finds that the many new agencies and organizations that emerged from it were difficult to administer at the local level. "The Cree have realized... that they have had imposed on them a network of new bureaucratic forms with overlapping functions and responsibilities...The important consideration from a strictly developmental perspective is that when organizations and agencies are not indigenous invention, then familiarity with them and gaining mastery over them will be more difficult" (Wertman, 1983: 287). The Cree had to cope with new administrations at the same time that they were faced with the confusion and trauma that followed large-scale dam construction. It should be little wonder, then, that the new regional administrations were not always models of efficiency and order and that their strategies for coping with self-destructiveness and violence were not always effective.

---

3. A more detailed presentation of such statistical material can be found in Niezen (1993a), the original published source for the figures presented here.

One of the most common sources of frustration with the formal system of handling behavior problems has been the tendency in the justice system to use punishment, usually incarceration, in response to family violence. This is seen to resolve none of the underlying issues, failing to achieve the goal of healing the emotional problems or addictions that are usually the ultimate cause of violence. A police officer in Chisasibi provided this observation:

> We get a lot of family disputes, domestic calls... usually it involves alcohol...and assaults... related to the alcohol. Usually people go to court for wife battery...I don't think that is the solution.... They keep coming back and they're doing it again, over and over...I think it would work if instead of taking them to the court, maybe in these kinds of events if there were some kind of healing. I don't think I would consider it healing taking a guy, putting him in prison for so long.

Another officer discussing the same problem with recidivism casually noted, "I arrested my brother I don't know how many times."

The handling of youth problems in the Cree communities is also controversial because it is still regulated by formal laws that approach behavior problems punitively. A common view is that the legal mechanisms involved in enforcing laws for youth protection and young offenders are too harsh, inclining toward punishment rather than compromise and reconciliation. As one elder observed, "When anything happens to one of our youth, you have to send them out to another place, Val d'Or or Montreal. And he gets into mischief and trouble. You have to send them out. I don't know why.... The medicine is not there that they're looking for. They need some kind of medicine, some kind of advice and instruction." What is referred to here is the advice once given more exclusively by elders. The new formal agencies could only offer counselling by educated professionals, without the all-important qualifications of age and wisdom acquired from connection to ancestors and experience on the land.[4]

The people most affected by relocation and loss of land are usually clear about the way it has affected their lives. The sense of irretrievable loss they describe is often similar to what might be experienced upon the death of a close family member; but with nearly everyone in the community feeling the same sorrow at the same time, the way to recovery is much more difficult. This observation is supported by the records of formal helping agencies which show especially high frequencies of depression, addictions, family problems, and juvenile delinquency during the decade following the start of hydro-electric construction. In the new, larger town of Chisasibi, informal methods of social control based on tolerance, forgiveness, and the diplomatic skills of elders, were overtaken by the rules and procedures of justice and social service programs. During the first years of implementation of the James Bay Agreement, these new agencies were both inefficient, with overlapping functions and inexperienced workers, and lacking legitimacy by being out of touch with local customs and expectations. The traumas associated with loss of land and relocation occurred simultaneously with an interruption in the process of healing.

Unfortunately, the James Bay Cree are not alone in being faced with such a crisis. Dislocation and resettlement are dominant themes running through many local histories of indigenous societies; and the social destruction resulting from the major events of 'development' are more a syndrome than an isolated occurrence. A recent global survey of mental health in low-income countries shows that the impact of displacement is one of the most significant causes of the social distress associated with high incidences of health problems, family violence, and self-destructive behavior. "Dam and re-settlement projects mean not only a loss of home and the identity that comes from a sense of place; they can obliterate generations of practical cultural knowledge and effort. To

---

4. See Niezen (1993b) for a more detailed exposition of Cree attitudes toward healing agencies.

this is added insecurity, nutritional deficiencies, sanitation risks, poor water supply, insufficient or infertile land, alcohol abuse, increased risk of illness, and barriers to health services" (Desjarlais et al., 1995: 138). Historical examples of this phenomenon abound in the literature on native North Americans. Anthony F. C. Wallace's ethno-historical study of the Handsome Lake religion of the Seneca, one of the 'Six Nations' from the Great Lakes region, for example, shows how settlement on reservations following the Treaty of Fort Stanwix of 1784 resulted in "slums in the wilderness." In these disenfranchised communities, alcoholism was rampant, resulting in "an explosive, indiscriminate hostility that vented itself in fighting even within the family" (Wallace, 1972: 200). Similar social conditions can be found wherever the insecurities of displacement occur. The relocation of Grassy Narrows, an Ojibwa community in northern Ontario, in the early 1960s for no other reason than to make it more accessible to modern services and amenities, is meticulously linked by Anastasia Shkilnyk (1985) with patterns of binge drinking associated with health risks, violence, neglect of children, depression, and suicide. The global nature of this phenomenon makes it all the more surprising that the social crisis following mega-project construction in the James Bay region was not anticipated.

THE PURSUIT OF HEALTH CARE AUTONOMY

The adjustments Cree administrators, political leaders, and their constituents were able to make to the implementation of regional autonomy had important consequences for developing the awareness and willingness among their members to engage in political action. Working to overcome the consequences of accelerated large-scale development at the local level was a form of public political education. Besides struggles to overcome the financial obstacles to implementation of programs under the James Bay Agreement mentioned earlier, there were steps taken to make existing services fit more consistently with Cree ways of perceiving things. Sometimes, as we will see, this involved unilateral action from a Cree administration to introduce new programs, making changes to existing programs, or breaking an established tie with a provincial agency. At other times it involved informal engagement in administrative programs at the local level, mostly by elders who perceived the 'white man's way of doing things' as inadequate. An increased sense of ownership of Cree administrations is part of a process of recovery from the emotional dislocations of environmental change and village relocation.

At the same time, administrative autonomy created a stronger sense of regional identity and a keener perception of threats to *iiyuu aaschi,* the 'people's land', preparing the way for broader participation among the Cree in responding to new hydro-electric projects and the perceived threat of Québec secession.

The main example of regional administrative development I will draw on is the Cree Board of Health and Social Services of James Bay. The legal parameters within which Cree health administrators were required to work in the early years of implementation of the James Bay Agreement left comparatively little room for the development of culturally appropriate policies and practices. For this reason, the cultural orientation of the Cree health board contrasts with the creative development of curriculum in the Cree School Board. The school board, as I will discuss below, wasted no time in building traditional curriculum into the services it was providing, including the exclusive use of the Cree language in the first three years of primary education (see Preston, 1979 and Salisbury, 1986).

The health board, however, did not develop a similar commitment to the promotion of local traditions but rather was compelled to work within a system that did little to accommodate Cree cultural distinctiveness (Association des Centres de Services Sociaux de Québec, 1986). Budget crises and restrictive laws governing such areas as confidentiality and the social patterns of fostering made it difficult or impossible to implement reforms that would make its services more culturally appropriate. This, Moffatt argues, is a situation that Cree administrators are going to have to live with: "the Cree do not really have self-government because they have to negotiate a budget annually with the provincial government. However this is a reality that is unlikely to disappear under any form of self-government" (Moffatt, 1987: 227).

Administrative oppositions were built into the new autonomous Cree health care system. In addition to maintaining ultimate control of operational purse strings, the Québec government established procedures and regulations in many aspects of health care and social services, including the criteria of medical qualifications and competence, confidentiality, fostering, adoption, the definition of 'young offenders', and procedures to be followed after their arrest. The Cree Board of Health and Social Services, in turn, was (and remains) financially and procedurally accountable to Québec's Ministry of Social Affairs.

Roistaing, writing of the Inuit's Kativik Regional Government established through the James Bay Agreement, finds similar impediments to formal cultural autonomy and states, "The important decisions affecting the territory's and the Inuit's development continue to be taken by the government in the south where political, economic and administrative power truly lie" (Roistaing, 1985: 23). The Cree Health Board must implement and enforce policies that have been legislated in the South, often without concern for the isolation and cultural uniqueness of northern native communities. The provision of medical services goes hand in hand with the enforcement of laws and procedures that often lack local legitimacy.

The implementation of regional autonomy in the administration of health care in Cree society is characterized by two conflicting cultural currents. Exclusivist tendencies in formal medicine were initially exacerbated by efforts to incorporate Cree health care within a provincial framework. In the first years of regional autonomy, medical services were deepening their influence in Cree culture, with little consideration of indigenous practices, through the development of new administrations coupled with imaginative uses of the technologies of health and communication.

At the same time, major development projects, the La Grande hydro-electric complex in particular, had given the

Cree people an awareness of the fragility of the forest way of life. This, in turn, has led local leaders to assess the threats to Cree culture and to adopt strategies for cultural protection. Missions and medicine have both been subject to scrutiny for the ways they may have eroded what are perceived to be important Cree traditions. Earlier Christian prohibitions against Cree ritual activity, especially drumming, are now commonly being called into question. Similarly, the expectation that a Cree board of health should take into account the unique cultural background of the constituents it serves is more often being expressed.

On the eve of the implementation of the James Bay Agreement during the late 1970s, the Cree population was facing two health-related challenges that were resistant to biomedical intervention: isolation in the forest and mental illness in the communities. A summary of some of the leading causes of death in Cree, native, and Canadian populations in the mid-1970s shows comparatively low mortality in the native and Cree populations for circulatory illness, cancer, and respiratory illness, but high mortality from accidents, poisoning, trauma, and suicide (Bernèche and Robitaille, 1980: 16). The Cree Board of Health and Social Services of James Bay, which took control of Cree health administration in 1981, inherited a medical system required to serve a young population (with more than 50 percent under the age of twenty), predisposed toward violent and self-destructive behavior.

The Cree Health Board also began to serve a population whose principal economic pursuits—hunting, trapping, and fishing in predominantly remote areas—were fraught with risk, not only from accidents that occur in the course of daily activity but, more importantly, from the remoteness of this activity from biomedical intervention. Isolation was seen, in itself, to be a medical problem.

'Bush kits' were one solution to the hazards of isolation in the forest lifestyle resulting from a perception of the inadequacy of healing in remote hunting camps. The bush kit program was implemented in 1982 by the Department of Community Health as a way to respond to medical problems being faced by hunters and their families in remote traplines.

This was to be a unique undertaking that went far beyond the "paper bag" of medicines provided informally in other northern communities. As a first step, Cree personnel were trained as first-aid instructors. Volunteer hunters were then recruited to participate in a week-long first-aid training course before taking responsibility for the health needs of hunting camps. By 1990 the program had recruited 210 volunteer 'lay healers' (a term used in the program's reports) from the community of active hunters (Lavallée et al., 1990: 190). First-aid kits containing a wide range of dressings, anti-inflammatory skin creams and ointments, antibiotics (eight types, oral and topical), pain-killers, antihistamines, a bronchodilator, an antacid, oral rehydration powder, and other medications, were approved by a board of doctors and dentists of the Cree Health Board (Lavallée et al., 1990: 190). A first-aid manual was produced for inclusion in the kits which describes in plain language the procedures to follow in emergencies, how to identify medical problems, and how to use the medications in the kit. The manual was partially intended as a guide to be followed during radio communication between the care providers of camps and village nurses (Lavallée, 1991: 6; Cree Board of Health and Social Services of James Bay, n.d.). All camps participating in the bush kit program had access to radio receiver-transmitters, provided since 1978 by the Cree Trappers Association, establishing a direct link with medical personnel in the communities who were able to provide advice and determine the necessity of air evacuations.

For those living in remote camps, the benefits of radio communication and bush kits are clear. The kind of medical emergencies that at one time cost lives or left people permanently disabled are more often treated successfully through air evacuations and hospitalization; and the combination of bush kit medicines and professional advice through radio networks has increased medical knowledge and resources in the camps. The effort to make health conditions in the camps consistent with those of the communities is an important source of formal support for forest life.

At the same time, however, the placement of medical services in the forest environment seems to have had an impact on the indigenous system of healing. Intuitively, some Cree people feel that traditional medicine has been eroded by the bush kit program because it acts to replace, rather than complement, healing grounded in the resources of the forest (Robinson, personal communication 1995). A formal evaluation of the bush kit program by Lavallée (1988) presents more concrete indications of such an impact. Healing strategies in this study are shown to vary according to the availability of bush kits. In response to the question, "What did the caretaker do for the patient," the dual use of traditional and biomedicine is clearly evident; but the presence of bush kits, only five years after the implementation of the program, is associated with a less frequent use of traditional healing, nearly 9 percent less than in camps without the bush kit (Lavallée, 1988: 43). Robbie Matthew, Sr. expressed to me the view that radio links to nursing stations can sometimes encourage dependency. He once overheard a message being relayed through the bush radio network from someone seeking advice from a nurse on how to treat a blister on his hand. Although the bush kit services are important, some feel they can also compromise the self-sufficiency of those in the remote camps if they are relied upon too much.

Helping agencies, especially health and social services, also face dilemmas with regard to the issue of confidentiality. One of the things that seems to bring some clients to the doors of doctors and counsellors is their trust in the rules that prohibit disclosure of anything they say. At the same time, however, this trust is incomplete. Clients or their families sometimes discuss sensitive matters with others in the community and then blame the formal agency for disclosing information when it later becomes public knowledge. Clients themselves often appear to be suspicious of files and lack confidence in the ability of offices to keep a written record of their personal affairs confidential. There is an apparent contradiction in the attempt to establish social relationships that are at the same time abstract (based upon formal rules and procedures) and personal (dealing with emotional and sensitive issues). In an earlier generation, an elder who provided counselling could usually be trusted to know when information had to be kept within limits. In this informal context, the relationship was based on face-to-face, oral interaction. In formal agencies, however, the coexistence of a potentially permanent, written record with a legal promise of confidentiality is sometimes seen as a frightening contradiction.

At the same time that legally-sanctioned confidentiality is mistrusted, it is also sometimes seen as an obstacle when family members feel excluded from important knowledge and events. Examples of such crises of confidentiality, as a Cree health worker noted, seem to be found most commonly in the formal medical system:

> In the law it says, a child [over] 14 can have an abortion without letting her parents know.... She could sign a paper and this could be arranged between the doctor and her. This happened...where a child had been flown out, and was losing a lot of blood. But the parents wanted to know what happened to their daughter. Then there was that collision of cultures, where the parents say, "She's still single, so we're still responsible for her and we need to know what happened." And the girl didn't want to tell them.

There is a contradiction in local attitudes toward confidentiality in Cree administrations that has affected their ability to work effectively: It is seen as untrustworthy when it is supposed to be dependable and too inflexible in its efficiency when it is supposed to adapt to individual circumstances.

The first years of implementation of the James Bay Agreement increased the formalization of medicine and social services, widening the distance between biomedicine and indigenous healing. At the same time, portable medical technology and links to medical personnel through radio and emergency air transport brought biomedicine into the remote forest setting. Although many hunters were and are deeply appreciative of these services, others have voiced concern over the impact of the bush kit program on the vitality of traditional healing practices and self reliance of those out on the land. In this new area of biomedical influence these expressions of gratitude and concern are reminiscent of contemporary, and perhaps historical, responses to the introduction of Christianity.

Such concerns have led to assessments of medical services which have a parallel with the reappraisal of Christian prohibitions. Elders are being informally consulted and formal programs assessed for their impact and cultural premises. These initial efforts are indicative of the potential for the Cree health board to move in a new direction. By pressing the issue of the cultural impact of important aspects of health care on many fronts, as it seems prepared to do, the Cree health administration may succeed in creating conditions that encourage dual use of traditional and formal medicine, thereby reinforcing the Cree system of healing as an important reference point for local identity.

REDEFINING EDUCATION

The Cree School Board, brought into existence through the James Bay Agreement, succeeded far more than the health board in adapting its programs to the local culture. The Cree Way project had already begun the process of grass roots curriculum development during the transition from federal control to Cree school administration (see Preston, 1979). Concerns with enhancing primary grade Cree language–curriculum were to continue under the new regional school board. The Cree Programs of the Cree School Board put together a series of primers for grades three and four depicting the routines of families engaged in subsistence activities in the forest, with titles like: *A Family at Bush Camp* (Cree School Board, 1991a) and *Setting Night Lines* (Cree School Board, 1991b). A series of lavishly illustrated books similarly oriented to the Cree way of life for grades one, two, and three was produced through the Modern Language Centre of the Ontario Institute for Studies in Education.

One of the limitations of the Cree Way project was a lack of linguistic research and material for Cree instruction in higher grades. This need was at least partially met by the

Cree School Board with the production of a *Cree Lexicon* (Cree School Board, 1987), the first major collection of Cree words ever published. The school board's Cree-English dictionary presents 60,000 words with four versions of each word: northern and southern dialect versions with both syllabic and Roman orthography. The central purpose of this project was wide distribution of a comprehensive dictionary for use in the school system by language instructors and teachers using syllabics, leaving the production of a more basic dictionary for student use to a separate project now under way (Daisy Herodier, personal communication, 1994).

An innovative curriculum is only one aspect of the Cree School Board's comparative success. Equally important is an unusually strong element of both formal and informal democracy in the school board's operation. Elders act as consultants in the production of new teaching material, and the community itself has significant input in assessing the suitability of curriculum to village needs. The committees of the Cree School Board are, according to Salisbury (1986: 129), active, influential bodies of village members who know one another, and the school administrators, very well. As Salisbury notes, unlike the school committees of southern Québec schools, Cree committees have significant authority: "A group may decide that a particular teacher is not teaching their children appropriately, or that a particular subject is not being taught the way they would like. They do not hesitate to make their feelings known to the school principal, and there have been several cases where a teacher's (even a principal's) contract has not been renewed, following a dispute with parents" (1986: 129). This kind of intervention in school affairs is not possible under circumstances in which teachers and principals are protected by union contracts. No such union, Salisbury reports, exists for employees of the Cree School Board. Yet what might amount to a disproportional amount of influence among parents in the Cree school system does not translate into discontent among professional teaching staff because, "Those working for the Cree School Board welcome the challenge to create new programs, at a time when their southern confrères are confined closely by the existing ministry programs" (Salisbury, 1986: 130).

The Adult Education Service is a new program that built upon the success of primary education in providing a bridge between Cree experience and the training necessary for formal employment. Between 1977 and 1982, Salisbury reports (1986: 123), 1,581 adults, roughly 25 percent of the Cree population aged eighteen and older, registered for courses with this program. The subject matter of these courses shows a range that reflects needs for training in both managed forest activities and burgeoning regional administrations, including snowshoe-making, economic development of bands, game wardenship, operation of outfitting camps, development of clerical skills, and methods of local administration, to name a few. The variety of its programs stems from the ability of the Adult Education Services to respond to requests by bands for training in particular fields by organizing teaching staff and funding.

The demand, by both sexes, for educational improvement is directly related to new opportunities for formal employment in Cree organizations. Women are sometimes the household breadwinners, mainly working in secretarial and service positions. The opening of a new day care facility in Chisasibi in 1993 reflects this increase in participation by women in the work force. The example of Violet Pachanos, the first female Cree chief and first female Deputy Grand Chief, shows that higher education is an important criteria for formal leadership in Cree administrations; and there seem to be significant cultural and practical disincentives for women to pursue educational goals in southern cities. This is a situation that may be at least partially addressed with the planned development of a college with programs for Cree students who would not have to leave the region to complete their training (*The Nation*, 1996a).

For men, the opportunities for employment have been different. Proportionately there are few positions of senior management, and these are mostly occupied by men who completed their formal education in the 1960s and 1970s. An educated strata, roughly estimated by Salisbury (1986: 75) to consist of some one hundred Crees, occupies the policy-making positions as senior members, chairmen, presidents, and directors of regional administrations, some individuals simultaneously occupying several appointments. They are, Salisbury concludes, "overloaded with activity...and they tend to meet with close acquaintances on different boards that cross-cut one another.... [T]here is a sense of common effort in a common enterprise, among a close-knit regional elite" (1986: 75). For most younger men, employment opportunities are spread through a wide range of agencies such as the Cree Trappers Association and the Cree Housing Corporation, Cree-owned businesses, of which only a few, like Cree Construction and Air Cree-bec, provide significant employment, and, in the southern communities, seasonal labor in mining and forestry.

For both men and women, a growing population threatens to out pace the availability of new opportunities. This presents a challenge to Cree educators who are trying to make college programs more accessible to youth and at the same time trying to find a way to handle the nearly 2,000 employed Crees who need further training or education and 600 adults trying to acquire a minimal level of literacy in English or French (*The Nation*, 1996a).

Despite its community-based structure and success in developing programs responsive to Cree needs, the Cree School Board still faces serious challenges. Cree education in the first three grades means that English or French (the choice is up to parents) becomes a second language in the middle of the primary program, a significant disadvantage for those who seek high academic achievement. Students whose parents are in the bush under the ISP program, and those attending secondary school outside of their communities are often temporarily fostered in Cree families. In October, 1991, eighty-six students in Chisasibi's secondary school were placed in temporary homes in a fostering program that costs the school board approximately $150,000 per year, for this community alone (Nancy Bobbish, personal communication, 1993). Although students are placed in familiar cultural surroundings, and sometimes among relatives, this is an experience that occasionally causes emotional problems among children and uncomfortable reminders among some adults of their years in residential school.

Such feelings, however, do not accurately reflect the changes that have taken place in Cree education since the early 1970s. Although hunters still have great prestige, and successfully living on the land is still an avenue for local leadership, there is an ever-growing awareness that formal education has distinct advantages, producing a new form of leadership that is more effective than the community of elders in managing local agencies, dealing with governments, and challenging industries that threaten Cree resources. The Cree have developed an educational system that carefully defines and communicates the values of forest life in the Cree language, then goes on to provide the foundation of knowledge and skills in the provincial curriculum. This has been central to the formation of an effective leadership and the creation of cultural bridges necessary for accommodation to a new social order.

ACCOMMODATION

The social crisis in Chisasibi cannot be said to have passed entirely. Charles Bobbish, elected Chief in August, 1995, saw alcohol abuse and its related social problems as one of the most important challenges he faced: "A lot of young people are starting to drink. There are hardly any activities organized for them and hardly any jobs for the young people" (*The Nation*, 1995b: 7). But his concern is with a generation that did not experience the trauma of relocation in the late 1970s, whose boredom and apathy are not complicated by the disruptions of roads, reservoirs, and removal. This was confirmed by a veteran tribal policeman who spoke to me in 1992 about the changes in police work he has seen in the new village: "I think I've seen changes for the better...for the first few years when we moved, the problems started getting worse...[with] parties going on for a week. Now we don't have those kind of parties, or people out drinking in the streets." Gone are the days when large groups of young people stayed up late into the night 'walking the road'.

It is simple enough to see the positive changes that occurred, but more difficult to explain what happened. The establishment in 1991 of a check-point for search and seizure of alcohol on the main road nineteen miles from the village has, some people say, had the effect of increasing sobriety; but bootleggers have found many ways of getting around 'the gate', including keeping a pit bull in the back of their car that the staff at the check-point was not prepared to deal with (a strategy that worked until the dog attacked someone in the village and had to be killed). Others have tried carrying alcohol overland, around the gate, a virtually unstoppable means of evasion in winter when people can travel almost anywhere by snowmobile, but more hazardous in summer when bootleggers sometimes found themselves stuck in peat bogs in the company of swarms of biting insects.

The process of accommodation to the new village was marked by community festivals which at least to some extent mitigated the problem of boredom mentioned by Chief Bobbish while restoring memories of life in Fort George. In the summer of 1988 the first annual *'mamoweedow minshtukch,'*[5] 'island gathering,' took place on Fort George Island. This was an event attended by hundreds of people from Chisasibi, other Cree villages, and towns in the South who crossed the La Grande River on large freighter canoes for several days of camping, feasting, square dancing, and a miscellany of other activities, such as archery contests and greased-pole climbing. Families attending the *mamoweedow* often set up teepees or prospector tents near the sites where they once had homes. The success of this event encouraged the inauguration of an annual pow-wow on Fort George Island a few years later which now attracts over 250 drummers and dancers from as far away as western Canada and the United States. Some young people in Chisasibi, awed by the costumes and performances of this event, have started

---

5. This is in a popular form of orthography, used on posters, T-shirts, hats, and other souvenirs of the event.

their own drumming group, the David Cox Memorial Drummers, and look upon it as an important part of their heritage, despite the censure of some Christian elders and skeptics who point to contrasts between the individual drumming and singing style of the Cree and the group performances of the 'war drums' used in the pow-wow circuit.

It is also from within regional native administrations created through the James Bay Agreement that the potential for cultural reform is beginning to be realized. The Cree Trappers Association, for example, has requested greater attention to traditional healing in the medical services provided in remote regions. In response to this request, bush-kits are being reexamined for their impact on traditional healing, ongoing research is recording and cataloging Cree healing methods to evaluate them for possible inclusion in the bush kit program, and provision of a manual of traditional medicine is being considered for use in the camps (Lavallée, 1991; Elizabeth Robinson, personal communication, 1995).

Active intervention in deficient provincial services is another strategy of administrative reform that has been used successfully. On August 1, 1994, for example, the Cree Board of Health and Social Services officially cut ties with the Centre d'Orientation L'Etape, a provincial establishment for troubled youth. Ten years of poor administrative relations between the Cree social services and L'Etape, aggravated by a failure of the Québec government to train and hire Cree youth counsellors for the facility, despite a $300,000 annual budget to do so, and an increase of runaway incidents confirming the inappropriateness of the existing services, prompted the decision to intervene. In a letter dated July 27, 1994 to L'Etape from Soraya Cote, the Director of Youth Protection for the Cree region, the provincial facility is warned that, "steps are immediately undertaken in order to repatriate all the budgets presently available to your centre for Cree Clientele," going on to state the Cree social service's intention to remove the young people currently assigned to the facility (*The Nation*, 1994: 16). As a temporary measure, the five youths removed from L'Etape were first moved to a group home in Mistassini, then flown to a bush camp run by

Chisasibi elder Robbie Matthew, Sr. who offered to provide them with an immersion in the forest-way of life.

In the provision of health care and social services one of the ways that a new spirit of cultural pluralism is being expressed is through the informal involvement of elders in difficult cases. Robbie Matthew Sr. told me about his intervention in the care of a youth diagnosed with severe mental illness:

> Last year the doctor told me, "We have a problem with a youth at the hospital."
>
> I never really knew what happened to this gentleman. He was married, had several children.... They had to take him to the hospital in Montreal, put him in an institution, hold him up there. But he didn't like that...I guess he had to get out. So the police caught up with him and really locked him up for escaping. They had to bind him when they sent him there, bind him so he couldn't move his legs and arms.... They had a lot of drugs [they gave him]: needles, pills, all kinds of drugs....
>
> "Well," I said to [the doctor], "How many years have you been dealing with this young man?"
>
> "Two, three years," he said.
>
> I said to him, "If he had medication its not working right for him. Maybe he needs some other kind of medication."
>
> What I meant was, there is a lot of medication being out on the land. Maybe he required some kind of medication being out there.... Finally we decided that we would have another round, see what really happens after we take off some of the medication... and when the next [meeting] came around, I told them, "If I'm right, we should put this young man into the bush. Take him off the medication. Give him a new start. And he could also see all the other camps, other camps on the highway. Maybe he could stay one day with friends or relatives. Take him out. Maybe he will have a different outlook, a different

feeling altogether. Because you've kept him in the hospital for too many months of the year...."

Anyway, this is what they did with this student. The hospital chartered a plane, took that guy to his family to take him out on the land. He was there for two months.... The next time I saw him was at the commercial center.... I said to him, "How was your trip?"

And he said, "It was very good. It was good for me, because I'm healed."

So that's what this healing process is all about.

Although the initial strategy of intervention in this case might be reminiscent of the institutional abuses of the 1950s, the inclusion of an elder in the consultation process and a willingness to implement his suggestions resulted in a different, more successful approach that reflected Cree helping-strategies. This example also illustrates one of the ways that sovereignty can be contested, or re-delegated outside of the formal political process. Far from the offices of band or First Nations governments, informal leaders can exert influence, altering the strategies of formal administrations to make them more consistent with local understandings of healing and social responsibility.

But not every elder is able to make such a contribution. The relationship between elders and youth is sometimes a source of misunderstanding and contention. People in their middle age and younger often see the elders' style of communication as alienating young people and contributing to their problems. Some elders in Chisasibi, for example, use the community radio to criticize the activities of teenagers, including their sexual behavior, in an effort to publicly shame them. The radio station provides them with access to broadcasting facilities out of respect but will sometimes cut them off as soon as they are seen to violate individual rights of confidentiality. However well-intentioned, not every informal effort to promote community healing receives widespread support or results in measurable success.

A form of adjustment to the rapid pace of social change that has only an indirect connection to community healing can be seen in the development of a more tangible sense of regional identity. One of the ways this occurred was though a new media network, linking the dispersed Cree communities. Local radio stations, such as the Chisasibi Telecommunications Association, in addition to playing music covering a range of tastes from heavy metal to gospel and country/western, broadcast regional news and narratives in the Cree language. Media development also occurred through the establishment in 1993 of a bi-weekly newspaper, *The Nation*, by a group of young Cree journalists based in Montreal. It was soon distributed and read widely throughout the James Bay region, with most articles in English and some in Cree syllabics. By far the most popular item in the early editions were its restaurant reviews, satirical descriptions of some of the infamous (and on rare occasions surprisingly good) greasy-spoon cafeterias of the North. Also popular are classified ads in which family members, often separated by school or work, send each other greetings. But more attention is being paid to its political reporting, which documents Cree responses to the activities of forestry, mining, and power industries as well as the successes and failures of Cree administrations and political leaders. If, as Benedict Anderson (1991) convincingly argues, the development of print-as-commodity contributed to the emergence of language-based national identity, the Cree are themselves well on the way to self-identification as a people with a common culture and common political aspirations.

Cree administrations are themselves another avenue for a stronger affirmation of regional identity, but only to the extent that there is a sense of 'ownership' of authority. The Cree Health Board, with its close ties to an outside expert culture and legal system, has taken a comparatively long time to begin the process of establishing anchorages to local understandings of the Cree way of life. Many of its services are seen to be important, sometimes inadequate only in the sense that there are not enough of them, but there is at the same time little perception of the health board as a distinctly 'Cree' entity. The school board, with its innovative primary curriculum in the Cree language, has been more active in defining, reifying, and communicating a regional cultural identity. And, as we will see in the next chapter, the Grand Council of the Crees, since its inception as a political watch dog during negotiation of the James Bay Agreement in 1974, has been an active, autonomous exponent of regional Cree political rights and the collective rights of indigenous peoples. Regional autonomy, in the sense that it is seen to represent 'Cree' interests rather than the assimilative strivings of non-native government, has created a stronger sense of the James Bay Cree as a distinct cultural entity.

6

Struggles over Sovereignty

It is making fools of people to tell them seriously that one can at one's pleasure transfer people from master to master, like herds of cattle, without consulting their interests or their wishes.
Jean-Jacques Rousseau *Political Writings.*

To an uninitiated observer at the United Nations Human Rights Summit in Geneva, Switzerland in June, 1993, the behavior of some members of the audience as the Canadian representative from the Department of Foreign Affairs spoke might have seemed puzzling: they were standing with giant placards marked boldly and simply with the letter 'S.' There were no words or other visible explanation of their meaning. Was this perhaps some sort of protest over money? But the vertical bar was missing. A form of short-hand for some key message of protest? Save the Whales? Self-determination? Sovereignty?

This line of reasoning would have been moving in the right direction, but the letter 'S' was intended for the end of a word, not the beginning: Canada, in discussing the rights of indigenous peoples, had refused to use the plural form of the word 'people' because of its implications in international law, which grants all 'peoples' the right of self-determination. Canadian delegates to the United Nations have suggested alternatives in the drafting of a Declaration on the Rights of Indigenous Peoples, including the words 'populations', 'communities', 'societies', or even 'people' in the singular. A curious aspect to this position is that Canada uses the standard terminology in its constitution, in which aboriginal 'peoples' have a distinct status. This was confirmed by a speech at the United Nations by Scott Serson, Deputy Minister of Indian Affairs, in which he explained that the use of the word 'peoples' in the Canadian Constitution was not intended to imply recognition of aboriginal rights under international law (in Coon-Come and Moses, 1996: 8). The battle over the 'S' involved Canadian governmental resistance to use of the word 'peoples' because it accords aboriginal peoples the right to self-determination. Indigenous groups, including the Grand Council of the Crees, insisted that it is a prohibited form of discrimination to deny a group the status of 'peoples' so as to prevent the enjoyment of rights that go along with that status (Coon-Come and Moses, 1996: 9).

On October 31, 1996 this seemingly intractable difference took a large step toward resolution. Indigenous delegates to the fifty-third session of the Working Group on the Draft Declaration on the Rights of Indigenous Peoples were surprised by a formal statement presented by representatives of Canada which included, "the Government of Canada accepts a right of self-determination for indigenous peoples which respects the political, constitutional and territorial integrity of democratic states" (Government of Canada, 1996: 2). The statement goes on to stress the importance of negotiations between states and indigenous *peoples* to determine the latter's political status and the strategies that can be used to pursue their economic, social, and cultural development.

This is only one example of a range of issues the Crees and other indigenous groups have successfully pursued through participation in international politics. The Grand Council of the Crees first went to the United Nations in 1981 to address unresolved grievances with the Québec and federal governments. As Grand Chief Coon-Come and Ambassador Ted Moses explain, "We went to the international community because we had come to the unhappy realization that there was little likelihood of solving our problems, grievances and differences by addressing ourselves exclusively to the Government of Canada or the Province of

Québec or by raising our issues only inside of this country" (1996: 2). As an illustration of such grievances, Coon-Come and Moses cite an epidemic of gastroenteritis that swept through the Cree communities in 1980, resulting in the deaths of eight children. They refer to epidemiological studies indicating that this epidemic would likely not have occurred if the specific sanitary infrastructure and service provisions of the James Bay Agreement had been implemented in a timely manner (1996: 2). The 1981 trip by Cree leaders to the World Health Organization and United Nations Office in Geneva was prompted by this instance of neglect which, more than other unrealized provisions of the Agreement, had immediate consequences for Cree lives.

From this moment on, Cree leaders, mostly those educated in high schools and colleges outside the Cree region in the 1960s and 1970s, have cultivated a prominent place as representatives of indigenous peoples at the United Nations. In 1987 they applied for and were granted consultative status by the Economic and Social Council of the United Nations, making the Grand Council of the Crees one of twelve indigenous peoples organizations worldwide to hold this position. This has allowed the Grand Council to work closely with United Nations organizations to promote international recognition of the rights of indigenous peoples. Cree representatives have attended a wide variety of international conferences with the goal of presenting aboriginal views, including a Habitat II Conference on housing in Istanbul, a World Summit on Food Security in Rome, and a Vienna Human Rights Summit. They maintain contact and work cooperatively with the European Community and European Parliament, the International Labour Office and the Organization of American States, as well as indigenous organizations from around the world (Coon-Come and Moses, 1996).

The Cree leadership has achieved a level of international recognition that allows it to use the politics of embarrassment with great effectiveness. Having acquired command of the strategies of international lobbying in pursuit of fair implementation of the James Bay Agreement, and formal representation on the United Nations Economic and Social

Council, the Crees have brought other major grievances to the attention of foreign governments and international agencies. When the Québec government decided to implement the second phase of the James Bay project with another massive network of dams, dikes, roads and transmission lines around the Great Whale River, the Crees went to the international community, especially the major buyers of Québec's power in New York City and the New England states, to bring attention to the negative consequences of earlier hydro-electric construction and the likely social and environmental impact of another mega-project. And when the Québec government began to actively pursue unilateral secession from the rest of Canada, the Crees waged an effective national and international campaign to publicize their sense of outrage that aboriginal rights to self-determination were being violated. In doing so, they likely had a significant influence on the outcome of Québec's 1995 referendum on sovereignty. These are two examples of the ways that a relatively small indigenous group can influence the fortunes of state agencies and national (or aspiring-to-be-national) governments.

THE JAMES BAY PROJECT REVISITED

In 1986 Robert Bourassa was returned to power as premier of Québec. Having had time outside of the premiership to consolidate his plans, he wasted no time in announcing his intention to complete the next stages in the James Bay Project. Two further phases, expected to cost a total of $48 billion, were proposed for the Great Whale River, further north than the La Grande, and the Nottaway-Broadback-Rupert River network (referred to as the NBR scheme) in the southern part of the James Bay region. The first part was to be a $13 billion hydro-electric project for the Great Whale River, with three new generating stations producing a capacity of some 3,000 megawatts. The dams, water diversions and infrastructure that would link this proposed new complex with the consumers in the South, were immediately seen by the Cree as a threat to the wildlife, habitat, and, by extension, the hunting-way of life. The reservoir expected from this second phase of the James Bay Project was to inundate 3,536 square kilometers (more than 2,000 square miles) of land (James Bay Energy Corporation, 1992), a fact that in itself raised concerns about its impact. By the mid-1980s, the Cree had already seen at first hand a wide range of unexpected consequences resulting from the La Grande project, including mercury poisoning, a decline in animal populations, and social disaster among youth in the villages.

In 1989 Cree claims that hydro-electric installations were affecting game received dramatic confirmation. A herd of 10,000 caribou were drowned on the Caniapiscau River (a tributary of the La Grande) when the spillway of a dam released an ill-timed torrent of water. Newspapers around the world displayed graphic images of the shores of the river choked with the bloating corpses of caribou, and most also cited the response of Hydro-Québec spokesmen who referred to the incident as an "act of God." The James Bay Coalition, an environmental lobby group, later took out a full-page advertisement in the *New York Times* called, 'Catastrophe at James Bay' which included a large photograph of the drowned herd (James Bay Coalition, 1991). Besides creating a prominent embarrassment for the utility and undermining arguments that hydro-electricity has minimal environmental consequences, the caribou drowning strengthened Cree resolve to stop James Bay II without compromise.

Having learned the limitations of fighting in the Canadian courts, the Grand Council of the Crees and leaders of the community of Great Whale began a public relations campaign in New York City and the New England states—the largest consumers of Québec's power. The campaign began with a striking idea, the construction of a canoe that represented a hybrid of Cree an Inuit designs, a symbol of solidarity between the two societies that would be most affected by the Great Whale project. Given the name 'Odeyak', combining Cree and Inuit words (*'uut'* and *'qayaq'* respectively), it was used to transport a rotating crew of some fifty Cree and Inuit volunteers who travelled from Ottawa, east to Montreal, down the Richelieu River to the Hudson and on to New York City. Along the way, Cree and Inuit speakers visited nearby communities. "We spoke in church basements, in high schools, wherever people would listen to us," recalls Matthew Mukash, then chief of Great Whale (in Greenwood, 1995). Snowballing media coverage of the voyage culminated on Earth Day, 1992, when Grand Chief Matthew Coon-Come addressed a crowd in Times Square. Introduced by then-mayor of New York City, David Dinkins, Coon-Come presented the message of Cree opposition to James Bay II, not only to the 10,000 in attendance but also to a much larger audience watching the evening news. Alluding to the heightened environmental awareness of Earth Day celebrants, Coon-Come concluded his speech by shouting, "today, you are all Crees!" to which the crowd responded jubilantly (Greenwood, 1995: 58).

Grand Chief Matthew Coon-Come addressing a rally in New York City, 1991. Photo by Gretchen McHugh.

Environmental lobby groups took up the Cree cause with alacrity. The Sierra Club, The National Audubon Society, and Natural Resources Defense Council were among the groups based in the United States that formed alliances with the Grand Council of the Crees. Environmental activists were instrumental in raising questions about the long-term impact of dam construction. Audubon senior staff scientist, Jan Beyea, anticipated the destruction of an ecosystem situated on the central flyway of most migratory birds in North America, and as large as California, if James Bay II were implemented. The new project, in her opinion, would "make James Bay and some of Hudson's Bay uninhabitable for much of the wildlife now dependent upon it" (cited in Kapashesit, 1991: x). Such concerns were an important part of a widespread growth of awareness about the James Bay project and the development of public skepticism about its ecological and social viability.

The Cree were also successful in globalizing their campaign against the Great Whale Project. In February, 1992 the Grand Council of the Crees was a plaintiff at the hearings of the second International Water Tribunal (IWT) in Amsterdam, The Netherlands. The IWT, sometimes referred to as the 'Amnesty International of water', was convening an international jury of experts to consider ten cases of possible violations of water rights from around the world, among them the James Bay Project of Québec. In its ruling, the jury referred to Canada's reputation as a country that respects human rights, and expressed surprise at the inconsistency between this reputation and the Canadian government's insensitivity to the rights of the Crees. The Tribunal also passed judgment on Québec's energy policies. Calling on provincial and federal governments and Hydro-Québec to seek alternatives to large-scale dam projects, the Tribunal advised that future energy policies be redirected to "reduce wasteful energy consumption rather than enlarging the capacity to generate energy" (Grand Council of the Crees, 1992: 9). Cree delegates were delighted at the Tribunal's findings: "The jury's ruling was a great victory for our people. The ruling was unambiguous and clear: the International Water Tribunal determined that the first phase of the

James Bay mega-project was imposed on the Crees, and that the devastating impacts on our health and the environment were never taken into account" (Grand Council of the Crees, 1992: 9).

In the spring of 1992 New York Governor Mario Cumo canceled a New York Power Authority contract with Hydro-Québec for the purchase of 1,000 megawatts of power; and two years later, New York dropped a seasonal contract for 800 megawatts that was up for renegotiation. These, and other potential contract losses in the New England states, intended to comprise some 10 percent of Hydro-Québec sales, seriously compromised the financial viability of the Great Whale Project (Maxwell et al., 1996: 12–13).

On November 18, 1994, premier of Québec, Jacques Parizeau, announced at a news conference that the Great Whale Project was being shelved. Parizeau's separatist Parti Québécois government had been in power for two months at the time of this announcement. Lobbying from environmental groups, cancellation of contracts in the United States, and censure from international organizations were not the only significant factors in this decision. The drive for Québec independence, the first priority of the Parizeau government, would not be helped with the Crees waging an effective campaign against the James Bay project in the United States. In a speech in Washington on the same day as Parizeau's announcement, Grand Chief Matthew Coon-Come had already shifted his attack from Great Whale to Québec secession, referring to Québec separatists as promoting an "ethnic nationalism based on ancestry and language" (1994a: 4), which does not have legitimate claim over northern Québec, yet holds to double standards by refusing to take into consideration the rights of native peoples to similar self-determination. Newspapers lauded Parizeau for his astuteness and good sense of timing in canceling the James Bay project. The *Montreal Gazette,* for example, offered this commentary on the decision: "Getting rid of Great Whale, in effect, pulls the rug out from under the Cree campaign; by shelving the hydro issue, Mr. Coon-Come no longer has a high-profile U.S. stage that he could use to lobby against Québec independence" (1994b). This, as we will see, was to seriously underestimate the adaptability and influence of indigenous political persuasion.

TWO SOVEREIGNTIES

Québec and the rest of Canada are locked in a repetitive constitutional stalemate that finds expression in futile negotiations punctuated by two unsuccessful referendums on Québec sovereignty, first under the provincial leadership of René Lévesque in 1980 and more recently, on October 30, 1995 under Jacques Parizeau, bolstered by a strong federal separatist party, the Bloc Québécois, led by Lucien Bouchard. The defeat of the 'Yes' side in the 1995 referendum by the narrowest possible margin, 49.5 percent 'No' to 48.7 percent 'Yes', was immediately followed by a vow from Bouchard to try again (without specifying when), suggesting a constitutional situation in which neither side can claim victory or find a stable solution.

The Crees and other Aboriginal people in Québec are in the middle of this Canada/Québec struggle. Cree leaders have expressed disquiet about the possibility of an independent Québec and have challenged the most recent unilateral referendum on sovereignty because of the *indépendantistes* failure to recognize northern natives as possessing equal or greater rights to self-determination as the Québécois. What has emerged from the Cree response to separatism were two conceptions of self-determination in Québec, aboriginal and Québécois; and the differences between them must in some way be resolved before Québec's place within or outside of Canadian confederacy can be definitively determined.

In *Nationalism and the Politics of Culture in Québec*, Richard Handler (1988) invokes the idea of 'cultural objectification' to explain the development of Québec nationalist ideology. For Handler, 'culture', as expressed, for example, by professional and amateur ethnologists, historians, and folklorists, can becomes perceived as a 'thing', an authentic natural object with well-defined traits. As a cultural object, nationalist ideology brings out sentiments of admiration, pride, patriotism, and a rejection of all others who do not show similar appreciation.

At the same time, there is some variety in the forms that objectified nationalist ideology is expressed. One of the salient features of Québec nationalist sentiment is permanent attachment to one's native soil. The land of one's birth becomes inseparable from one's character, both as an individual and as a Québécois people who share a common ancestry. This is in part derived from the perception that in the colony of New France: "The soil protected and nourished the nascent collectivity, providing the material necessities of life and promoting those moral virtues associated with uncorrupted labor and a pastoral milieu (Handler, 1988: 33–34).

Closely associated with attachment to *la patrie* (the homeland), then, is a shared code of conduct that suggests how one must act in order to be Québécois. Cultural content for this code of behavior is derived from history, from the general accounts of the origin and development of Québécois culture. One of the more interesting expressions of this normative cultural construction comes from the idea that New World geography, climate, and cultural interaction influenced the early French settlers to create the foundations of the Québécois nation of today. Contact with American Indians, usually perceived as the "ecologically pure noble savage", are among these 'natural' influences reported by Handler (1988: 37).

The dark side of Québécois nationalist ideology is the negative vision, the idea of cultural integrity threatened by corruption and dissolution from outside forces: "[F]or modern nationalists, as for their predecessors, the perception of ongoing political, cultural and linguistic assimilation gives rise to major fears. American culture and the English language are sometimes seen as irresistible in their power to seduce individuals away from their natal traditions and to invade the national territory itself, corrupting the Québécois people against their will" (Handler, 1988: 49).

But American culture and Canadian confederation are not the only threats of cultural pollution and death. Handler's idea can be extended to include competing cultures within Québec's own borders. Among these cultural rivals, the native peoples of Québec, who have failed to assimilate; who pursue rival political objectives; whose bilingualism is usually in aboriginal languages and English; who have, in short, their own, potentially rival version of an objectified culture; and who present one of the most potent threats of loss of identity, the negation of boundaries, and, ultimately, the disappearance of the Québécois nation. This might explain why Parti Québécois candidate Richard Le Hir raised controversy by disparaging the culture of the Québec Crees: "I would have something to learn from them if it could be shown that their culture demonstrated its superiority in one form or another.... [But] when you look at what heritage has been left by native civilizations—if you could call them civilizations—there is very little" (*The Gazette*, 1994a: A13). Indians of yore may have been among the cultural influences that created Québécois identity, but the Indians of today are among the perceived threats to its continuity.

These ideological principles are attached to one overriding political ambition: the realization of a national political boundary that corresponds with ethnic attachments to the 'homeland.' For the Parti Québécois leadership, this means making a distinct nation out of the current province of Québec, including northern territories that the federal government signed over to the province in 1898 and 1912. David Cliche, Parti Québécois liaison with Québec's native people, made it clear that an independent Québec will have the same borders as the province: "What is not on the table is the division of the territory of the province of Québec and the eventual division of the territory of Québec as a state" (*The Globe and Mail*, 1994a: A2). This view was reinforced with a veiled threat from Jacques Brassard, Parti Québécois Minister of the environment, that an independent Québec would resist any native separatist attempts "with the means of the modern state" (*Globe and Mail*, 1994b: A1). Québec separatists have at least been clear about one thing: the boundaries of their nation would be the same as those of the current province of Québec, despite the cultural distinctiveness of the people in its vast northern territories.

Cree ideas and ambitions of self-determination are very different from Québécois nationalism, although appearances may sometimes indicate otherwise. The Cree, in common with other aboriginal groups in Canada, refer to themselves as a 'First Nation;' seemingly to reinforce the notion of aboriginal peoples having an inextinguishable claim to sovereignty, the Cree administrative office in Ottawa is called an 'embassy,' and their representative at the United Nations Economic and Social Council is an 'ambassador.' These simple facts point in the direction of an aboriginal 'proto-nationalism,' the construction of an identity attached to a claim for statehood. It would be a mistake, however, to use these facts as a basis for the assumption that the Cree leadership is pressing for a form of nationhood that would include complete political autonomy, separate currency, control of well-defined borders, and full membership in the United Nations General Assembly. Rather, the goals of Cree sovereignty are oriented towards formal recognition and guarantees of self-determination within an already-existing state—Canada. The Crees are pursuing autonomy without nationalism, self-governance that does not include control of an ethnically-defined state.

This goal seems to be easily misunderstood. Whether through ignorance or manipulation of national and international opinion, Parti Québécois leaders have raised the false specter of indigenous peoples in other parts of the world following the (as they see it) Cree example of pursuing aboriginal separatism. David Cliche, for example, said, "If the Crees in Québec go their own way, the next will be natives in British Columbia, and then the Ojibwa in Northern Ontario, and eventually every native nation on three continents" (*Globe and Mail*, 1994a: A1). The idea of a spreading fire of indigenous nationalism quickly dissipates, however, when we consider the fact that self-determination for the Cree means the choice of *inclusion* in an existing state, not autonomy in the form of a breakaway aboriginal state.

This is not to say that Cree perceptions of sovereignty are grounded in a relationship of dependency with the federal government. Those who live on the land in particular often express pride in an ability to be self-sufficient, to survive, if they had to, without paper money or the help of formal agencies. As an elder from Chisasihi stated, "Never [wonder] where you are going to get something that you can eat tomorrow [or think that] you cannot eat unless you have money. Out on the land there is a lot of richness, a lot of nourishment that is free for the taking. Why can't we go out on the land where everything is free?" This clear and simple expression of the ideal form of autonomy does not take into account the complexities of federal and provincial relationships with aboriginal peoples, nor does it recognize the need for strategies to resist the encroachment on Cree territory of extractive industry, but it does express succinctly the kind of autonomy that Cree political leaders have devoted themselves to protecting. As Grand Chief Matthew Coon-Come remarked in an address to the Center for Strategic and International Studies in Washington D.C., "We have always conceived of ourselves as one people, tied together by the land we share and care for, and upon which our survival has always depended. We Crees are not 'nationalists'. That concept does not exist in the Cree language. Our tie to the land is not just political, it is also physical. We are part of our lands" (1994b: 2).

The government of the Crees and the separatist government of Québec have expressed agendas for self-determination that are fundamentally different and, without significant change of direction from either side, on a potential collision course if Québec continues to pursue independence. The Cree goals for self-determination, partly realized and partly compromised in the James Bay Agreement, involve protection of rights to land and of the forest economy, guarantees of continuing support for village-based services such as education, health care, and municipal infrastructures. Additionally, the Cree hope for a degree of political and administrative autonomy that would allow Cree leaders to, first of all, choose affiliation with Canada or a sovereign Québec, and secondly to develop administrative policies and programs that are intended to be consistent with the cultural uniqueness and geographical isolation of the North.

The separatist government of Québec has as its goal national independence for all its present provincial territory. Included in its intended assumption of state control are all treaty obligations and all fiduciary and administrative responsibilities toward native peoples. It would also assume all responsibility for review and approval of development projects in the North. What the Crees see as forcible and illegal inclusion of aboriginal peoples in an independent Québec, the sovereigntists see as legitimate control of territories that belong to *'la patrie,'* destined to be a free and sovereign nation.

'THE SPOILERS'

On June 20, 1991 the National Assembly of Québec enacted a law, *an Act respecting the process for determining the political and constitutional future of Québec* (Bill 150), to prepare the way for a constitutional referendum, possibly leading to establishment of a sovereign Québec state. The intervention of federal/provincial negotiations leading up to the constitutional agreement referred to as the Charlottetown Accord superseded Bill 150; but the Accord was not ratified, and in 1994, the election of a sovereigntist Parti Québécois government in Québec, led by Jacques Parizeau, brought the issue of Québec secession back to the forefront. Parizeau soon called for a unilateral declaration of independence, the sole prerequisite for which was a vote in favor of this action by a majority of Québec voters. The date of October 30, 1995 was set for this referendum on Québec independence.

In principle, the Cree leadership has not been opposed to national independence for the Québécois. "The Cree people understand and respect the cultural and political aspirations of Québecers, at least with respect to lands that are legitimately theirs," says Grand Chief Matthew Coon-Come (1995: 1). The central theme of Cree objections to Québec's sovereignty movement is its denial of Cree claims to self-determination, and failure to recognize Cree attachments to their land and distinctiveness of lifestyle. "We Crees do not think of borders as sacred. We are part of the land. There is no other place in the world where everything, every hill, every stream, every fork in the river is named in Cree," (1995: 3), remarks Matthew Coon-Come, pointing to the strength of Cree attachments to land that neither Canadian nor Québec governments seem to have recognized in debates leading up to the 1995 referendum.

The Québec government's record of failure to consistently recognize the importance of cultural uniqueness among

First Nations peoples seems to have a particularly sharp edge, providing one of the reasons behind Cree unwillingness to support Québec independence. An event that has stuck in the minds of many native people is the handling of a protest in 1977 in the Inuit community of Kuujjuaq (formerly Fort Chimo) against the Parti Québécois government's proposed Charter of the French Language (Bill 1). Left unchanged, this bill would have forced Cree and Inuit community and regional administrations to use French, no doubt severely affecting the ability of native administrations to function, while adding another element to cultural destabilization. Twenty-five policemen from the Sureté de Québec were flown to Fort Chimo as a show of force to quell the Inuit protest. Responding to critical press coverage of this incident, and perhaps to arguments by aboriginal spokesmen that the language bill contravened the terms of the new James Bay and Northern Québec Agreement, changes to Québec's language Bill were negotiated. The language rights of Crees, Inuits, and Naskapis were recognized and corresponding exemptions to the language legislation were made. The threat of the use of force by the Québec government to enforce language legislation, however, has not been forgotten, nor has the apparent double standard by which Québec took steps to become unilingual while requiring indigenous people in the northern regions of the province to become trilingual, in aboriginal language, English, and French (Grand Council of the Crees, 1995: 153–155).

Another feature of Québec separatism that seems to have disquieted the province's aboriginal people is the apparent ethnic exclusivism of the campaign for sovereignty. The more extreme edge of Québec sovereigntists sees the nascent nation as a culturally bounded entity that particularly favors the 'pure laine,' (pure wool) Québécois. But even the Parti Québécois leadership has expressed such sentiments. While still a member of the opposition, Jacques Parizeau made a statement that seemed to exclude minorities and native peoples from the project of Québec sovereignty: "Québecers can achieve the objective they have set for themselves even if, for the most part, those who vote for it are almost exclusively Québecers of old stock" (*The Gazette*, 1995b: B-3). Grand Chief Matthew Coon-Come, explaining the reasons behind the negative attitudes of the Québec sovereigntist leadership toward Cree claims to cultural uniqueness and rights of self-determination, could find no answer other than the fact that it resulted from, "a discrimination we can only conclude is based on race" (1994b: 4). With exclusivism as one of its starting points, the *indépendantistes* stand little chance of winning over Québec's aboriginal people.

The real substance of Cree opposition to inclusion in an independent Québec is the Cree leadership's stark portrayal of double standards in Québec's sovereigntist agenda. Grand Chief Matthew Coon Come, in an address to a Conference of the American Council of Québec Studies, stated what proved to be the most effective argument against the indivisibility of a sovereign Québec: "If Canada is divisible because of Québec's right to self-determination, why, then is Québec not divisible as well?" (1994a: 4). The same point has been echoed by Doran in expressing his fear of the possibility that Canada would fragment into multiple break-away states as a result of Québec separation: "Québec ultimately must confront the paradox of sovereignty. If Canada is divisible, then why is Québec indivisible? If Québec is indivisible, then on what grounds should Canada be obliged to allow Québec's secession?" (Doran, 1996: 104). The use of this argument by Québec's First Nations becomes, for Doran, more evidence of the potential for Canadian balkanization, increasing speculation that both Canada and Québec would fly apart with the centrifugal forces of a successful vote for Québec separation. Doran fails to note however that the Cree did not vote 96.3 percent in favor of a breakaway aboriginal state, but against any separation of their people and territory from Canada. As the report, *Sovereign Injustice,* commissioned by the Grand Council of the Crees, states, "[T]he James Bay Crees and other Aboriginal peoples in Canada are not seeking to secede from Canada. However, they are seeking clear and unequivocal confirmation of their right to self-determination. Faced with the threat of a unilateral declaration of independence by Québec, Aboriginal peoples seek to exercise their right to choose to remain in Canada" (Grand Council of the Crees, 1995: 62). Despite a long history of ambivalence toward policies and programs resulting from federal involvement in aboriginal affairs, the intervention of native people in Québec's bid for sovereignty was directed toward Canadian unity, a preference for alignment with the federal government.

With organized resistance to the Great Whale hydroelectric project well under way when Parizeau announced his intention to pursue the sovereignty issue, the Cree leadership already knew how to proceed leading up to the October, 1995 referendum. As early as 1991, the Grand Council of the Crees had begun consulting legal, constitutional, and political advisors, in particular Paul Joffe, a lawyer and legal scholar specializing in aboriginal human rights. Their task was to consider the implications of Québec's constitutional differences with the rest of Canada, from a position, "consistent with Cree perspectives, policies and positions [while endeavoring] to place the Grand Council of the Crees in the most informed and advantageous position to defend the rights and status of the James Bay Cree people, regardless of the outcome of the Québec secession question" (Grand Council of the Crees, 1995: v). The study resulting from this consulting project was submitted to the United Nations Commission on Human Rights at its forty-eighth session in 1992, giving the Crees the advantage of an early start in bringing international attention to their concerns about Québec independence.

Another political strategy used by the Grand Council of the Crees leading up to the 1995 Québec referendum was the implementation of a Cree referendum on inclusion in a sovereign Québec one week before the provincial vote. On October 24, 1995, voting stations were opened in schools or meeting halls in all nine Cree communities as well as towns and cities outside of Cree territory with significant 'expatriate' populations: Montreal, Val D'Or, Senneterre, Ottawa, and North Bay, Ontario. The Cree referendum faced logistical difficulties because in late October the hunting season was under way and many families were out on the land. Those living in road-accessible camps drove to polling stations, sometimes from hundreds of miles away. Cree families in remote territories were also given the opportunity to vote. They were contacted by radio, asked to provide their coordinates and to stay in their camps between October 20th and 24th. Three helicopters were chartered to fly thousands of miles to over one hundred camps, giving remote hunting families the opportunity to participate in the Cree referendum. Under these conditions, 4915 Crees, over 77 percent of eligible voters, participated in the vote. The result was unambiguous: 96.3 percent voted 'No' in response to a question which asked if they consented as a people to be separated from Canada and included in an independent Québec (*The Nation*, 1995d: 5; Coon-Come, 1995: 2–3). At the same time, other First Nations peoples in Québec took similar action. The Inuit and Innu (or Montagnais) also held referendums, with similar results: 'No' in more than 90 percent of the votes (Coon Come, 1996: 13).

The timing of these aboriginal referendums was such that they had the greatest impact possible on the Québec referendum. Just days before Québec voters were to decide the issue of sovereignty, the Parti Québécois leadership, with the momentum in its favor, was faced with a serious challenge to the territorial integrity of an independent Québec. Their choice was to acknowledge that Québec can itself be divided, or to deny claims to self-determination by native peoples. By digging in their heels on the potential divisibility of Québec, they could be seen as holding to a double-standard on self-determination: Canada can be divided to accommodate the nationalist aspirations of the Québécois, but Québec itself cannot be divided to accommodate the clear will of the Cree and other native people of the North to remain with Canada.

Not long after the 1995 Québec referendum, the Grand Council of the Crees sponsored a survey which indicates the possible effectiveness of the aboriginal claim to self-determination. A study conducted independently by Insight Canada Research, which surveyed 686 Québecers and 538 Canadians in other provinces on the question of Québec separation shows that two-thirds of Québecers agree that the northern Cree and other aboriginals have a right to remain in Canada with their lands if Québec separates. Even among Québec's francophone community, the main source of the separatist movement, 57 percent took the position that aboriginals have a right to keep themselves and their lands in Canada (*The Gazette*, 1996a: A-12). This means that by drawing attention to the double standards of the sovereigntist leadership and insisting on their rights being recognized, native leaders in Québec have the potential to sway as much as 7 percent of the Québécois electorate away from the 'Yes' vote. It also means that such an effect may already be present in the results of the October, 1995 referendum, that Cree and other aboriginal strategies may have been a significant part of the final outcome.

While it is impossible to determine with certainty the reasons behind voter response to the sovereignty issue in Québec, the very close result of the 1995 referendum suggests a highly unusual political event: the actions of a relatively small number of aboriginal people were among the decisive factors in (temporarily at least) maintaining the political unity of an industrial nation. When the first Québec referendum on sovereignty failed to pass in 1980, the Crees of Mistassini were occasionally subject to verbal abuse in the town of Chibougamou, where Québec separatists called them, among other things, 'spoilers,' classifying them among those who helped to stand in the way of Québec nationhood. But following the 1995 referendum, in the light of such a narrow margin of defeat of Québec secession, the epithet might have been more accurate.

As in the campaign against the Great Whale hydroelectric project, Cree resistance to forcible inclusion in a sovereign Québec also attracted important supporters. Christos Sirros, former Québec Indian affairs minister and currently Liberal Member of the National Assembly (Québec's provincial legislature), concurred with Cree arguments that Québec is divisible and the James Bay Agreement cannot be unilaterally altered by a separatist government: "Natives are not migratory birds, they are not things that can be transferred from one jurisdiction to another. They are human beings who have a relationship with two governments. It is inconceivable that one government can unilaterally change that" (*The Gazette*, 1995c: A-4). Ron Irwin, federal Minister of

Indian Affairs and Northern Development, not long after the close sovereignty vote of October, 1995, voiced greater support of the Cree position than any federal representative had ever done before, and even raised a storm of controversy by predicting bloodshed if Québec were ever to try to force its native territories to leave Canada following a vote for sovereignty. The Parti Québécois leadership responded to Irwin's remarks with outrage. Jacques Brassard, Québec intergovernmental affairs minister said, for example, "Either Mr. Irwin is an irresponsible arsonist who is lighting fires everywhere in a dangerous way or he is an ignoramus who is uttering nonsense" (*The Gazette*, 1996b: A-2).

But these seem to be isolated voices. The federal government has not, to this point, acknowledged the outcome of the 96 percent Cree referendum vote to remain with Canada. Less than one month after the Québec referendum, Cree officials were angered by the federal government's attempts to water down the notion of aboriginal self-determination in a draft declaration from a United Nations working group on the rights of indigenous peoples meeting in Geneva. "This is the thanks we get," said Ted Moses, spokesman for the James Bay Cree, "It's as if there was no referendum and no year-long debate in Québec and the Cree didn't demonstrate their rights" (*Ottawa Citizen*, 1995: A-4). An explicit federal position on the place of aboriginal self-determination in the possible secession of Québec was apparently never to appear, seemingly out of fear that First Nations will someday either want to secede from Canada, or that such recognition would encourage potentially expensive claims of land rights and regional autonomy.

Such government support of native self-determination no longer seems so far away. One year after the 1995 Québec referendum, Canada changed its position in the battle over the 'S.' By finally recognizing the right to self-determination of indigenous 'peoples,' the government of Canada has opened the door for a change in its relationship with the Cree and other native peoples who claim rights over land and self-government. A negotiated process of transference of a wider range of political powers and responsibilities than the Cree now have is a possibility inherent in Canada's new position in the United Nations Draft Declaration on the Rights of Indigenous Peoples. But do the positions taken by government representatives at international forums have an influence on domestic policies concerning indigenous peoples? Will meaningful negotiations result from this concilatory language? The way such negotiations might be carried out in the context of Québec claims to sovereignty and jurisdiction over native affairs is a question with far-reaching implications.

7

Conclusion

*I can only share with you, to tell you how we dealt with prob-
lems long ago. I cannot tell you...this is the way you have to
deal with it. For today, as leaders, workers, [problem solvers, life
solvers] you are faced with more new complications that touch
every aspect of our native culture...[Y]ou'll find many times it
seems so difficult...especially in dealing with life when two cultures are in conflict...clashing together...You'll realize in time
that life is not long. It seems short.*

Joab Bearskin, as heard,
interpreted and understood by Irene House.

The James Bay Cree have come to represent a new form of
society based upon an unusual relationship with bureaucracy.
Although the intention behind developing Cree administrations was greater inclusion in the policy framework and ideas
of the state, something quite different has unintentionally
arisen. It involves the largely successful deployment of segmentary politics within an aspiring nation-state geared
toward administrative and cultural homogeneity, a situation
in which an actor can side with an immediate kin-based
group, a village, a 'Cree Nation' or a country, depending upon
circumstances and inclinations. As Michael Herzfeld writes,
"In the modern nation-state, such shifting among levels of
solidarity is inconceivable. One's personal interests are sup-
posedly both subordinate to, and yet coincident with, those of
the state" (1992: 113). The Cree have developed responses to

the state's striving for inclusion of marginal groups, responses that go beyond the extremes of fatalism and violent resistance. By accepting the realignment of state agencies as much
as possible on their own terms, Cree leaders have been able in
large measure to neutralize them, strip them of their normative content, make them as much an avenue for Cree identity
formation as inclusion in an empowered Québec.

Regional autonomy is the device that makes this trick
possible. Attaching the prefix 'Cree' to the title of administrative agencies like the school board or health board raises
expectations that they will truly reflect local or regional
identity, not just parody the policies and attitudes of southern agencies though Cree incumbents. The process of indi-
genization has a built in fail-safe mechanism: if a policy or
program does not meet local expectations it is often a perfectly understandable product of state intrusion, 'white
man's thinking;' and within the limits of local lobbying, in-
ternal administrative reform, and in extreme cases, political
resistance, steps are usually taken to achieve a sense of ownership. Through this steady accumulation of reforms, Cree
administrations have become a kind of civil society with
teeth, a check on the propensity of the state to homogenize
language, culture, even, in some instances, techniques of enforcement.

Among the clearest illustrations of indigenous politics
acting as a check on state ambitions are in the Cree responses to two major crises: hydro-electric development and the
potential for forced inclusion in an independent Québec.
For Bourassa's Liberal government, the pride and national
character of Québec was best expressed through feats of engineering. The North was seen to be a resource-rich area
that could unify the province both as a geographical and
cultural entity when Québecers had physically conquered it
and constructed their monumental projects. Cree lobbying
in the United States and international forums was a significant part of the background to a shelving of the Great Whale
project and a repositioning (at least for the time being) of
Québec on the value of large dams.

The Parti Québécois rejected the notion of mega-projects
and aimed more directly at Québec national unification

through secession from Canada. The pride of Québecers was expressed through cultural and political struggle. Economic considerations were what might be called a priority of secondary importance, relevant only in so far as they impacted the potential viability of Québec as an autonomous state. The first goal was, and remains, independence; but the northern regions of the province were included in this ambition by Parti Québécois leaders without compromise, even though their constituents tended to be more understanding of claims by native people to an equal or greater attachment to land, language, and a distinct way of life. For the separatist leadership, the indivisibility of the nation-to-be, whether out of a perceived need to include northern resources within the new state, or an attachment to boundaries well under a century old, was an indisputable foundation of the drive toward secession.

This was a threat that mobilized the Grand Council of the Crees in a way that closely resembled the campaign against James Bay II, and that drew upon its experience. The Cree were obviously not alone in opposing Québec secession, but their part in encouraging the 'No' vote was pivotal. Again, the actions of indigenous organizations were an important part of an historic event, in confining the control of an aspiring state over their interests.

But political ingenuity has its limits. Even the leadership of the Grand Council, defending Cree territory against the potential destructive impact of large-scale projects and in dealing with constitutional crisis, could not become directly involved in the process of community healing. At best, a well-directed, peaceful political resistance can lead to greater assurance of the future viability of a way of life, to protections against the arbitrary will or neglect of industry and centralized governments; but the burdens involved in responding to the effects of relocation and environmental destruction were given more to local agencies and individuals. After the destruction following hydroelectric construction, the flooding of lands, relocation of villages, and highly accelerated institutional change, it became the task of Cree administrators to make the adjustments necessary for the viability of community life.

Elders and other informal local leaders were quick to point out the inadequacies of formal systems and to suggest alternative strategies more consistent with their vision of the past and understanding of the values of forest life. Although some personal efforts to resolve local problems, such as those made by elders chastising young people on community radio, exacerbate tensions more than overcome them, elders have also been an invaluable resource. They have been influential, for example, in the handling of a psychiatric patient, or in pointing to the inadequacies of the bush kit program. They have certainly been consulted for advice on the curriculum in Cree-language primary education, and they have sometimes volunteered as mentors to young people struggling with village and urban life and wanting to learn more about living in a camp, hunting and trapping for subsistence, and the strategies for developing a spiritual connection to the land. The reform of administrative policies and programs has taken place through a local process, through the influence of the segmentary allegiances and values of informal forest-based and village-based leadership.

We have seen in a concrete way how cultural convergence can lead unintentionally to a strong element of diversity, how social change patterned on Euro-Canadian institutions can lead to redefinition of tradition through administrative reform. New forms of knowledge in some circumstances can be used to define and defend a way of life based upon animal spirituality and subsistence in the forest through hunting, trapping, and fishing. This did not occur when control was monopolized by outside agencies. Residential schools, for example, cannot be said to have made a significant effort to incorporate local lifeways in their curriculums and teaching styles, at least not when they were driven by goals of assimilation. When the Cree people themselves were given some measure of control over formal institutions, a strong element of social disjuncture could be overcome by a countervailing process of identity formation. Whereas schools once had the task of eradicating 'heathen' traditions and preparing the Indians for a useful role in 'civilized' society, they could under Cree authority use literacy and formal methods of instruction to reinforce knowledge of language, values, and even subsistence techniques.

This new form of society is not based upon a synthesis of bureaucracy and tradition in the sense that administrations themselves take on aspects of local customs in an almost picturesque (if one is distanced from the consequences) style of inefficiency. One of the unusual things about Cree administrations is the degree to which they work, albeit not always perfectly, even in circumstances of geographical isolation and cultural distinctiveness. Achievements like the Cree referendum—using helicopters, bush radios and a wide network of support to implement an organized vote—are not within the creative or logistical abilities of many regional administrations. The Cree have developed a form of administrative culture in which relatively efficient bureaucracies can be used to define and defend an aboriginal way of life situated in the practice of forest-based subsistence.

Autonomous native administrations have a significant potential to alter the direction of state control, to resist the process of assimilation. In response to the cultural pressures of extractive industry and increased contact with native cultures elsewhere, leaders and constituents of Cree administrations are beginning to redefine identity and assert the importance of local traditions. Their criticisms and reform of such things as social service policy, medical programs, or school curriculums are not so much oriented toward a denial of the value of bureaucracy or technology as much as they assert a pluralism that recognizes the value of a dynamic Cree culture. By pressing for a recognition of cultural uniqueness in the development and application of local programs, the Cree are developing another dimension to political diversity in a western democracy.

References

Anderson, Benedict
   1991.   *Imagined Communities: reflections on the origin and spread of nationalism* London: Verso.

Anderson, David
   1854.   *The Net in the Bay; or Journal of a Visit to Moose and Albany.* London: Thomas Hatchard.

Anderson, J. W.
   1961.   *Fur Trader's Story.* Toronto: The Ryerson Press.

Association des Centres de Services Sociaux du Québec
   1986.   'Les nations autochtones et les services sociaux: vers une véritable autonomie', *Recherches amérindiennes au Québec, 16* (1): 51–69.

Bernèche, Francine and Yvonne Robitaille
   1980.   'Mortalité et morbidité Hospitalière de la population du territoire Criô, 1975–1977'. Département de Santé Communautaire, Hôpital Général de Montréal. Unpublished report.

Blacksmith, Kenny
   1995.   'Testimony of Deputy Grand Chief Kenny Blacksmity of the Grand Council of the Crees (of Québec) to the Joint Energy Committee, Massachusetts State House—March 23, 1995'. Unpublished paper.

Bourassa, Robert
   1985.   *Power from the North.* Scarborough: Prentice-Hall Canada Inc.

Brightman, Robert
   1993.   *Grateful Prey: Rock Cree Human-Animal Relationships.* Berkeley: University of California Press

Bruchac, Joseph
1993.   *The Native American Sweat Lodge: History and Legends.* Freedom, CA: The Crossing Press.

Buckland, A. R.
1894.   *John Horden, Missionary Bishop: A life on the Shores of Hudson's Bay.* London: The Sunday School Union.

Ciaccia, John
1991.   'Philosophy of the Agreement', in *James Bay and Northern Québec Agreement and Complementary Agreements.* Québec: Les Publications du Québec.

Coon-Come, Matthew
1994a. 'Energy, the Environment, Politics, and Native Rights'. Paper presented to the Conference of the American Council of Québec Studies, Washington, D.C.
1994b. 'The status and rights of the James Bay Crees in the context of Québec secession from Canada', Address to the Center for Strategic and International Studies, Washington, D.C., 19 September.
1995.   Remarks of Grand Chief Matthew Coon-Come to the Canadian Club. March 13, Toronto, Ontario.
1996.   'Remarks of Grand Chief Matthew Coon-Come', Harvard Center for International Affairs and Kennedy School of Government, October 28.

Coon-Come, Matthew and Ted Moses
1996.   'Canada and Circumpolar Cooperation: Meeting the Foreign Policy Challenge', Statement by the Grand Council of the Crees to the Standing Committee on Foreign Affairs and International Trade, Canada Parliament, 3 October.

Cree Board of Health and Social Services of James Bay
n.d.   'Bush Kit Manual'. Unpublished document.
1993.   The Mercury Newsletter. April.

Cree Hunters and Trappers Income Security Board
1991.   'Annual Report'. Sainte-Foy, Québec.

Cree School Board
1987.   *Cree Lexicon: Eastern James Bay Dialects.* Mistassini: Cree Programs of the Cree School Board.
1991a. *Tikwakuhch ka nituu piyaasuwaahwamaahch.* Chisasibi: Cree Programs of the Cree School Board.
1991b. *Ka kuschaayaahch nuuhtaawii a pipuhch.* Chisasibi: Cree Programs of the Cree School Board.

Cree Trappers Association
1989. *Cree Trappers Speak.* Chisasibi: James Bay Cree Cultural Education Centre.
1994. 'Annual Report, 1993–1994', Val d'Or, Québec.

Crighton, Michael
1990. *Jurassic Park.* New York: Ballantine Books.

Cronon, William
1983. *Changes in the Land: Indians, Colonist, and the Ecology of New England.* New York: Hill and Wang.

Desjarlais, Robert, Leon Eisenber, Byron Good, and Arthur Kleinman
1995. *World Mental Health: Problems and Priorities in Low-Income Countries.* Oxford: Oxford University Press.

Diamond, Albert
1988. 'The Costs of Implementing the Agreement', in Sylvie Vincent and Garry Bowers (eds.), *James Bay and Northern Québec: Ten Years After.* Montreal: Recherches amérindiennes au Québec.

Doran, Charles
1996. 'Will Canada Unravel?', *Foreign Affairs, 75* (5): 97–109.

Emerson, Ralph Waldo (Bliss Perry, ed.)
1995 [1926]. *The Heart of Emerson's Journals.* New York: Dover Publications, Inc.

Feit, Harvey
1985. 'Legitimation and Autonomy in James Bay Cree Responses to Hydro-Electric Development' in Noel Dyck (ed.), *Indigenous Peoples and the Nation-State: Fourth World Politics in Canada, Australia and Norway.* St John's: Institute of Social and Economic Research, Memorial University of Newfoundland.
1991. 'The Construction of Algonquian Hunting Territories; Private Property as Moral Lesson, Policy Advocacy, and Ethnographic Error', in George Stocking (ed.). *Colonial Situations: Essays on the Contextualization of Ethnographic Knowledge.* Madison: The University of Wisconsin Press.

Francis, Daniel and Toby Morantz
1983. *Partners in Furs: A History of the Fur Trade in Eastern James Bay 1600–1870.* Kingston and Montreal: McGill-Queen's University Press.

Gagnon, Y.
1989. 'Physicians' Attitudes toward Collaboration with Traditional Healers', *Native Studies Review, 5*(1): 175–186.

Gardner, James
1981.   'General Environment', in June Helm (ed.). *Subarctic.
         Handbook of North American Indians*, Vol. 6. Washington
         D.C.: Smithsonian Institution.

The Gazette (Montreal)
1992a.   'Cree itching to take charge of James Bay Project: Hydro,'
         13 February: A6.
1992b.   'Great Whale Spells Envoronmental Disaster', 20 March:
         A3.
1994a.   'Le Hir's harsh views on Natives raise eyebrows', 6
         August: A13.
1994b.   'Shelving Great Whale a wise move', 21 November: B2.
1995a.   'Indians Cling to Land, Treaty Rights', 2 April: A4.
1995b.   'World opinion a factor in aboriginals' planning', 2 April: A4.
1995c.   'Out of Step with Minorities' 10 April: B3.
1996a.   'Cree have a right to stay in Canada if Yes side wins: poll',
         25 January: A12.
1996b.   'War of words rages over Irwin', 15 February: A2.

Gellner, Ernest
1983.   *Nations and Nationalism*. Oxford: Basil Blackwell.
1988.   'Academician Ol'Derogge', *Africa, 58* (4): 480.

The Globe and Mail (Toronto).
1994a.   'Crees will have no friends, PQ negotiator warns', 19
         October: A1-A2.
1994b.   'Stay or go, our choice too, Crees say', 15 October: A1.

Gordon, Deborah R.
1988.   'Tenacious Assumptions in Western Medicine', in M.
         Lock and D. R. Gordon (eds.), *Biomedicine Examined*. Dor-
         drecht: Kluwer Academic Publishers.

Government of Canada
1981.   *Indian Acts and Ammendments, 1868–1950*. 2nd ed. Depart-
         ment of Indian and Northern Affairs.
1996.   'Articles 3, 31 & 34'. Unpublished statement to the fifty-
         third session of the working group on the United Nations
         Draft Declaration on the Rights of Indigenous Peoples,
         Geneva, October 31.

Government of Québec
1976.   *The James Bay and Northern Québec Agreement*. Éditeur offi-
         ciel du Québec.
1984.   'Act and Regulations Respecting Youth Protection'.
         Québec: Les Publications du Québec.

Grand Council of the Crees
1992. '1991–92 Annual Report'.
1995. *Sovereign Injustice: Forcible Inclusion of the James Bay Crees and Cree Territory into a Sovereign Québec.* Nemaska, Québec.

Greenwood, John
1995. 'The Vision of Matthew', *The Financial Post Magazine,* April: 33–36, 57–59.

Gregory, David
1989. 'Traditional Indian Healers in Northern Manitoba: An Emerging Relationship with the Health Care System', *Native Studies Review,* 5(1): 163–173.

Handler, Richard
1988. *Nationalism and the Politics of Culture in Québec.* Madison: The University of Wisconsin Press.

Herodier, Daisy, Elsie Duff, and Marianne Pash
1992. 'Dominant Cultures Influence on the Cree Way of Life (Community: Chisasibi)' Cree School Board, unpublished report.

Herzfeld, Michael
1992. *The Social Production of Indifference: exploring the symbolic roots of Western bureaucracy.* Chicago: The University of Chicago Press.

Hydro-Québec
1989. 'James Bay: Development, Environment and the Native Peoples of Québec'. Montreal: Unpublished paper.

James Bay Coalition
1991. 'Catastrophe at James Bay', advertisement, *The New York Times,* 21 October: A15.

James Bay Energy Corporation
1988. *La Grande Rivière: A Development in Accord with its Environment.* Montreal: Société d'Energie de la Baie James.
1992. 'Les superficies inondées'. Unpublished document.

Kapashesit, Winona LaDuke
1991. 'Foreword,' in Boyce Richardson's, *Strangers Devour the Land.* Vancouver: Douglas & McIntyre.

Kleinman, Arthur
1980. *Patients and Healers in the Context of Culture: An Exploration of the Borderland between Anthropology, Medicine, and Psychiatry.* Berkeley: University of California Press.

In press. 'What is Specific to Biomedicine?" in *Writing at the Margin: Discourses between Anthropology and Medicine*. Berkeley: University of California Press.

Lavallée, Claudette
1988.　'Evaluation of the Bush Kit Program', Department of Community Health, The Montreal General Hospital. Unpublished report.
1991.　'Faisabilité d'inclure des éléments de medecine traditionelle dans le programme bush-kit'. Département de santé communautaire, Hôpital Général de Montréal. Unpublished report.

Lavallée, Claudette, Hermes Cornejo, Catherine James, and Elizabeth Robinson.
1990　'The Eastern Cree Bush-Kit Program Evaluation: Its Usefulness', *Arctic Medical Research, 49:* 189–194.

Lechky, Olga
1991.　'Transfer of Health Care to Natives Holds Much Promise, Lecturers Say,' *Canadian Medical Association Journal, 144*(2): 195–197.

Locke, John (Peter Laslett, ed.)
1988　[1690]. *Two Treatises of Government*. Cambridge: Cambridge University Press.

Long, John S.
1985.　'Rev. Edwin Watkins: Missionary to the Cree: 1852–1857', Papers of the Sixteenth Algonquian Conference. Ottawa: Carleton University.
1986.　'The Reverend George Barnley and the James Bay Cree', *The Canadian Journal of Native Studies, 6*(2): 313–331.

MacGregor, Roy.
1990.　*Chief: The Fearless Vision of Billy Diamond*. Markham, Ont.: Penguin.

Magonet, Gordon
n.d.　'Treating the Cree: People of a Different Culture', in Helen Bobbish Atkinson and Gordon Magonet (eds.), *The James Bay Experience: A guide for health professionals working among the Crees of Northern Québec*. Government of Québec, Department of Health and Human Services.

Mala, Theodore A.
1984.　'Alcohol and Mental Health Treatment in Circumpolar Areas: Traditional and Non-Traditional Approaches', in Robert Fortuine (ed.). *Circumpolar Health* 84: Proceedings

of the Sixth International Symposium on Circumpolar Health. Seattle: University of Washington Press.

Maxwell, James, Jennifer Lee, Forrest Briscoe, Ann Stewart, and Tatsujiro Suzuki
1996.   'Locked on Course: Hydro-Québec's Commitment to Mega-Projects', unpublished paper, MIT Center for International Affairs.

McDonnell, Roger
1992.   'Justice for the Cree: Customary Beliefs and Practices'. The Grand Council of the Crees (of Québec)/ Cree Regional Authority. Unpublished report.

McNeill, W. H.
1976.   *Plagues and Peoples.* Garden City: Anchor Books.

Moffatt, Michael E. K.
1987.   'Land Settlements and Health Care: The Case of the James Bay Cree', *The Canadian Journal of Public Health, 78*(4): 223–227.

Moore, Thomas
1947   [1518]. *The Utopia of Sir Thomas Moore.* Roslyn, N.Y: Walter J. Black, Inc.

Morantz, Toby.
1978.   'Practiques religieuses des Cris de la Baie de James aux XVIIIe et XIXe siècles (d'après les Européens). *Recherches amérindiennes au Québec, 8* (2): 113–122.

The Nation (Chisasibi)
1994.   'Operation Liberation: Crees take troubled kids out of problem-plagued Val D'Or youth centre', 12 August, 16–17.
1995a. 'My father healing a broken leg, as told by Job Bearskin', 14 April: 11.
1995b. 'New Chief stresses value of Church', 6 October: 7.
1995c. 'Briefs', 6 October: 7.
1995d. '96.3% say No in Cree referendum', 3 November: 5.
1996a. 'Cree CEGEP finally in the works', 19 January: 5.
1996b. '150 Jobs for Crees?', 26 April: 7.
1996c. 'Sawmill approved with conditions', 19 July: 7.

Niezen, Ronald
1993a. 'Power and Dignity: The Social Consequences of Hydro-Electric Development for the James Bay Cree', *Canadian Review of Sociology and Anthropology, 30*(4): 510–529.

⟶ 1993b. 'Telling a Message: Cree Perceptions of Custom and Administration', *The Canadian Journal of Native Studies, 13* (2): 221–250.

In press. 'Healing and Conversion: Medical Evangelism in James Bay Cree Society', *Ethnohistory, 44*(3).

Ottawa Citizen
1995. "Ungrateful' government upsets aboriginals.' 17 November: A4.

Preston, Richard
1979. 'The Cree Way Project: An Experiment in Grass-Roots Curriculum Development', Papers of the Tenth Algonquian Conference. Ottawa: Carleton University.
1988. 'James Bay Cree Syncretism: Persistence and Replacement', Papers of the Nineteenth Algonquian Conference. Ottawa: Carleton University.

Richardson, Boyce
1991. *Strangers Devour the Land.* Vancouver: Douglas & McIntyre.

Roistaing, Jean-Pierre
1985. 'Native Regional Autonomy: the Initial Experience of the Kativik Regional Government', *Études Inuit Studies, 8*(2): 3–39.

Rousseau, Jean-Jacques (C. E. Vaughan, ed.)
1915. *The Political Writings of Jean-Jacques Rousseau.* 2 vols. Cambridge: Cambridge Unversity Press.

Salisbury, Richard
1986. *A Homeland for the Cree: Regional Development in James Bay 1971–1981.* Kingston and Montreal: McGill-Queen's University Press.

Scott, Colin
1988. 'Property, practice and aboriginal rights among Québec Cree hunters', in Tim Ingold, David Riches, and James Woodburn (eds.). *Hunters and Gatherers 2: Property, power and ideology.* Oxford: Berg Publishers Limited.

Shkilnyk, Anastasia
1985 *A Poison Stronger than Love: the destruction of an Ojibwa community.* New Haven: Yale University Press.

Speck, Frank
1977. *Naskapi: The Savage Hunters of the Labrador Peninsula.* Norman: University of Oklahoma Press.

Tanner, Adrian
1979. *Bringing Home Animals: Religious Ideology and Mode of Production of the Mistassini Cree Hunters.* Memorial University of Newfoundland, Institute of Social and Economic Research, Social and Economic Studies No. 23.

Thistle, P. C.
1986. *Indian-European Trade Relations in the Lower Saskatchewan River Region to 1840.* Winnipeg: University of Manitoba Press.

Trigger, Bruce
1985. *Natives and Newcomers: Canada's "Heroic Age" Reconsidered.* Kingston and Montreal: McGill-Queen's University Press.

Waldram, James B.
1990. 'Access to Traditional Medicine in a Western Canadian City', *Medical Anthropology, 12*(3): 325–348.

Wallace, Anthony F. C.
1972. *The Death and Rebirth of the Seneca.* New York: Vintage Books.

Weber, Max (H. H. Gerth and C Wright Mills eds.)
1948. *From Max Weber: Essays in Sociology.* London: Routledge & Kegan Paul.

Wertman, Paul
1983. Planning and Development after the James Bay Agreement. *The Canadian Journal of Native Studies, 3*(2) 277–288.

Willis, Jane
1973. *Geniesh: An Indian Girlhood.* Toronto: New Press.

Wolf, Eric R.
1982. *Europe and the People Without History.* Berkeley: University of California Press.

Young, T. Kue
1988. *Health Care and Cultural Change: The Indian Experience in the Central Subarctic.* Toronto: University of Toronto Press.